CONTENTS

HORRIBLE HISTORIES

VILLAINOUS VICTORIANS

TERRY DEARY

ILLUSTRATED BY **MARTIN BROWN**

■SCHOLASTIC

For Ben and Sam Goakes – who are not villainous Victorians
(well, they're not Victorians.) TD

To Richard Smith, for all the no worries. MB

Scholastic Children's Books,
Euston House, 24 Eversholt Street,
London, NW1 1DB, UK

A division of Scholastic Ltd
London ~ New York ~ Toronto ~ Sydney ~ Auckland
Mexico City ~ New Delhi ~ Hong Kong

First published in the UK by Scholastic Ltd, 2004
This edition published 2010

ISBN 978 1407 11775 1

Printed in the UK by CPI Bookmarque, Croydon

2 4 6 8 10 9 7 5 3 1

Introduction

History is horrible. People in the past did dreadful things to one another and committed terrible crimes. They still do.

But by the 1800s the laws had become even more cruel than the crimes! If you were caught chopping down someone else's tree you could be hanged!

The laws became so cruel you could feel just as sorry for the villains as for the victims! The prisons were full of poor people who pinched pennies by picking pockets.

Posh people didn't have to mug and murder to make money. They owned the filthy factories and murky mines where the poor slaved and suffered. Many mine owners didn't mind how many died in their damp and gas-filled pits as long as they themselves made lots of money.

So, in the dark days of Queen Victoria, who were the *real* villains? The poor, pilfering people of the slums? Or the mean, miserly men in their massive mansions? And how would YOU have got on in those terrible times?

Teachers may tell you Victoria's Britain was an exciting place…

IT WAS A TIME OF NEW INVENTIONS AND TERRIFIC DISCOVERIES

But it was also a time of cruelty and wickedness.

What you need is a book that tells you the other side of the story – the *villainous* Victorians. Now, where will you find a book like that…?

Terrible timeline 1830s-1840s

1837

In July 1837 a seriously weird artist, Robert Cocking, jumped from under a hot-air balloon to test a parachute. Robert was 61 years old in 1837 – quite a wrinklie at that time. His parachute looked like an umbrella when it's blown inside out. It was made to carry his weight – 90 kilos. Sadly Robert *forgot* to add on the weight of the parachute itself, another 110 kilos.

SO... A PARACHUTE MADE TO CARRY 90 KILOS IS CARRYING...

200 KILOS! HMM... THIS SHOULD BE INTERESTING

Robert had a drink of wine, took off his coat and climbed into the basket under the parachute. A hot-air balloon carried the whole thing 1.5 kilometres into the air over London.

He called up to the balloon pilots…

Brave Bob pulled a rope and let the parachute go. He fell towards Greenwich in London. He fell very fast. The stitching that held the parachute was a bit feeble. The basket fell off and Robert was smashed on the ground like a hedgehog on a motorway.

And it was…

And crackers Cocking was crocked.

In July 1837 a seriously weird woman called Victoria became Queen of Britain. Queen Victoria became famous for saying, 'We are not amused.' But though she never said it, she did write in her diary, 'We were very much amused.'

Tubby Victoria reigned for another 63 years and – even though *she* didn't do a lot – the last 60 years of the 1800s are known as the 'Victorian' age. So her name is remembered.

'Victorian' men and women like Brave Bob went round the world, doing daring and daft things. They risked their lives so that people like you and me can live in a different world. (Well, SOMEBODY had to try things like parachutes so today's airmen can fly safely.)

But while brave (though batty) people like Robert Cocking are forgotten,[1] un-brave (though fatty) people like Victoria are remembered.

Is that fair? No. Most history books tell you about the famous and the fortunate – there are a few thousand of them. But most history books *don't* tell you about the forgotten and the failures. There are millions of them. Yet we can learn just as much from the failures as we can from the famous!

It's time someone wrote about the real people in Victoria's world. A world full of wild, wacky wonderful people like Robert Cocking as well as vile, vicious and villainous people like Jack the Ripper. So here are some of the famous and fortunate along with the forgotten failures because it takes both to make real history…

[1] Robert Cocking is buried in St Margaret's Church, Lewisham, London, if you fancy going along to say 'thank you'. Look for the grave marked: 'Robert Cocking whose parachute detached from the Great Nassau balloon in 1837'.

1838 ━━━━━━━━◆━━━━━━━━

Isambard **Brunel** builds the first steamship to cross the Atlantic, while railways take people all the way from London to Birmingham. Brits are going places fast – but with lots of choking sooty smoke. Brunel himself almost choked on a coin that he swallowed doing a children's magic show. He invented a machine to turn himself upside down and shake it out.

William Lovett creates the 'Charter'. The 'Chartists' want votes for all men (but not women, of course). They get a great petition together and take it to Parliament. But Parliament throws it out and Lovett ends up in prison. He came out and tried selling books but that didn't make him any money. Neither did teaching or writing school books. He died in poverty.

1842 ━━━━━━━━◆━━━━━━━━

Thomas **Arnold** dies and he was only 47. He is one of the few people ever to become famous for being a teacher. He taught at Rugby School – a school where the senior boys had been teaching the younger boys how to riot. Spoilsport Arnold

Billy **Bean** shoots at the Queen – but his gun has more paper and tobacco stuffed into it than gunpowder. Then on 29 May **John Francis** fired at Her unpopular Highness and missed. He went back the next day and fired with an

put a stop to that. Terrible Tom Arnold also brought in the teaching of French (foul) and mathematics (miserable). Blame him.

empty pistol (couldn't afford the powder). Neither is executed and Queen Victoria is furious. Billy and John – forgotten failures.

1843

Charles **Dickens**, the writer, is having a bad time. His latest book, *Martin Chuzzlewit*, is not a huge hit and he is running out of money. Will he have to give up writing novels and get a proper job? No, because this year he writes the best-selling blockbuster *A Christmas Carol*. Everyone is saved – Dickens, Scrooge and Tiny Tim!

Frances **Evans** is a Welsh preacher's daughter. She leads rioters into the Carmarthen workhouse, where Frances and the poor people of the town have been suffering. Soon soldiers arrive and batter them. All the rioters want is 'Better food, free tools and freedom'. Not a lot. The riot doesn't do much good.

1848

Thomas Babington Macaulay writes a big fat history of England – so blame him for your history tests. He says England is gradually getting better – for him maybe! He says he isn't too bothered about any mistakes in his writing. So he'd never pass his SATs tests then.

Father MacIntosh is a good Scottish priest. The Irish Famine is remembered but people forget that Scots suffered at the same time when their potatoes rotted and they starved. Lord Cranstoun at Arisaig doesn't care about his clan. Hero MacIntosh is left to help them. Many die anyway.

Cruel criminals

When Victoria was Queen the poor workers of Britain were crowded into dark, damp and filthy little houses. (Well, the houses were handy for the foul factories that belched out choking smoke; the factories that paid them a pitiful wage. So the workers suffered the slums.)

But one class of people liked the dingy streets and black back lanes – the criminals. The slums were home to Whizzers, Van-draggers and Screws.

You don't know what they did? Oh, very well, I'll tell you. Whizzers picked pockets, Van-draggers stole from the backs of horse-drawn vans and Screws burgled houses.

The really villainous ones carried squirters ... no, not water pistols, you dummy. *Real* pistols!

No, no, no! A 'bogie' was a policeman.

Now here's a word you really needed to know if you were going to survive Victoria's England...

13

Gruesome garrotters

In the 1850s and 1860s a new terror hit the city streets – garrotting. A Victorian villain explained to our *Horrible Histories* reporter…

What did half of these villains do when they weren't robbing people in the alleys?

a) They were cab drivers.
b) They were teachers.
c) They were policemen.

A newspaper reported: 'London is a battlefield of raging cabmen.'

By 1863 there were 115 garrotting cases in London and other cities in Britain were starting to copy. Of course there were always 'honest' people who made money out of people's fear. In the 1860s a new type of men's clothing appeared…

Putrid punishments

Of course, the villainous Victorians couldn't be allowed to get away with their vicious crimes. When they were caught they were punished … and I mean PUNISHED.

Would you nab a 'kettle and tackle' if you could be whipped for it?

Here's a report of one beating from Leeds Jail.

V R

Her Majesty Queen Victoria's Jail - Leeds

Date: 3 January, 1867

Prisoner: Thomas Beaumont, age 47

Crime: Garrotting and robbing Abraham Dickenson of Batley near Dewsbury

Sentence: Five years in prison, 24 lashes

Report: The criminal was first strapped to a triangle of wood. The officer used a new cat-of-nine-tails whip - a whip with nine strands and three hard knots at the end of each strand. Beaumont took the first stroke in silence. After the second he cried out in pain and after the third he cried, 'Oh, dear me!' As the blows followed quickly his cries grew louder. After 12 strokes his back began to show marks from the lashing. By the end of the lashing he was screaming for mercy.

And you thought detention was bad?

Cruel to criminals

Victorian punishments could be a bit harsh, even if the villain was a child. If you were lucky, though, you'd just be fined.

Some of these fine crimes are true and some are false. Can you tell the fine-crime from the fake…?

PARISH NOTICES

1. Racing your dog along the street (and betting on the winner).
2. Being cheeky to a teacher.
3. Snowballing.
4. Forgetting to do your homework.
5. Sliding on the pavement.
6. Eating a pork pie after 9pm.
7. Being a man but dressed in women's clothes.
8. Laughing in school.
9. Shaking a carpet in the street after 9am.
10. Putting your tongue out at your dad.
11. Dumping your dead cat in the road.
12. Coughing in church.
13. Throwing orange peel on the pavement.
14. Eating sweets in class.

Lost:
Black cat
called
Tiddles

...rish
...eeting
...rsday
...pm

...cuss
...lem
...rance
...the
...ts

Found in
High st
– black
fur hat –
flat and
v. smelly

Answers:

1 True. Three boys who trespassed on a man's land were each fined just one penny but racing your dogs on the road would cost you a pound.

2 False.

3 True. Snowballing really could get you a fine back in Victorian times.

4 False.

5 True.

6 False.

7 True. James Wilson got away with a fine of two shillings and six pence (12p) for dressing as a woman.

8 False. Being happy in school wasn't a crime, but being happy in the street could be! In 1873 Peter McKenna was fined £2 for whistling, singing and dancing in the street.

9 True.

10 False.

11 True. You could be fined up to £5 for dumping a dead animal, rotten meat or poo in the street.

12 False.

13 True. Throwing orange peel cost one young man a 12p fine in 1873 – and it's still a crime today. (So is being drunk in charge of a horse and cart, which cost someone £1 in the 1860s.)

14 False.

Putrid prisons

Putrid prisons were for more serious crimes. Were these punishments fair? Or foul?

- In 1846 William Cleghorn killed Michael Riley in a boxing match and went to prison for six months.
- In 1873 Thomas Clark sent a chimney sweep lad up a 30-centimetre-wide pipe where the boy suffocated to death. Clark got six months in prison.
- In 1875 Isabella Reilly went to prison for *seven* years for stealing a purse with £10 in it. Isabella was 19 years old.

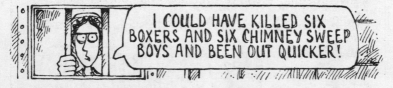

- William Lee stole a dress that had been put out to dry and got a whipping as well as two months in prison.
- Eleven-year-old Ellen Woodman was part of a girl gang caught stealing scrap metal. She was sent to prison for seven days.

Horribly hard labour

When convicts went to prison they didn't just sit around and chat. They had to work – taking thick, rough, used ships' ropes and untwisting them so the material could be used again. The work often made their fingers bleed.

But it was even tougher when the judge sent them to jail with 'hard labour'. Sometimes this meant breaking stones with a hammer. And if there weren't any stones to be broken, the prisoners were often given silly jobs just to exhaust them. Jobs like…

SHOT DRILL

Prison Life Weekly

Our reporter has been inside Pentonville Prison to see the conditions there. He is happy to report those evil men are really suffering. If you've ever had your pocket picked or your house burgled then you'll be glad to see this, dear reader.

Here is the sort of punishment a man can expect if he is sentenced to hard labour.

1 There are three lines of men. At the end of each line is a pyramid built from cannonballs. Each ball is as heavy as a sack of coal.

2 The man on the end must lift a cannonball off the top and put it down. The next man must pick it up.

3 So each cannonball goes along the line. The last man puts it down at his end of the line.

21

4 This goes on until the pyramid has been built at the other end of the line. Once that has been done, they begin to move it back again.

5 This goes on and on, backwards and forwards for an hour and a quarter. By this time the men are quite worn out.

Maybe they will remember this next time they think about stealing your wallet!

A reporter said the men worked till they sweated. A few seconds' rest might be allowed but mostly the prison warders shouted and bullied the men to keep going. A warder said...

The hardest part is picking the cannon-ball up. There's nothing to get hold of and their hands are slippery with sweat so it's like a greasy ball. The work makes the shoulders very stiff too.

Makes your PE lessons look easy, doesn't it?

Anyone who failed to do the 'shot drill' could be sent to work 'the crank'. That is, turning a handle on a machine – a handle that a strong man could turn once every three seconds. But in Birmingham Prison the punishment was to turn it ten *thousand* times. Even a fit man would take over eight hours to finish.

THIS IS A WIND-UP

Prison pain

Young criminals would also be set to work on the crank. If they failed they were...

- fastened into a straitjacket;
- tied, standing, to the wall of their cell for four to six hours.

If they fainted they had a bucket of cold water thrown over them.

I CAN'T WORK THE CRANK JUST NOW, I'M A BIT TIED UP

This happened to one boy called Lloyd Thomas three days in a row. Lloyd was ten years old. Another boy, Edward Andrews, refused to work the crank. He was punished for two months before he managed to hang himself. Edward was 15 years old. No one was punished for the cruelty that drove Edward to kill himself.

The crank was last used in 1898.

Fry and Fry again

One woman, Elizabeth Fry, led the fight to make 1800s prisons less cruel. In Preston Prison the treadmills were replaced with weaving looms so the prisoners could do some useful work. Good idea? Not everyone agreed.

Some people fought against her. They said prison *should* be tough.

The Reverend Sydney Smith, for example, argued that…

But Mrs Fry slowly made changes. Thanks to her there were:

- separate prisons for men and women;
- different punishments for serious and not-so-serious crimes;
- useful work and training;
- better food, warmth and clothing for all.

PAH! THAT WOMAN OUGHT TO BE LOCKED UP!

But it's Liz Fry who is famous and remembered, while savage Syd is forgotten.

Cruel to kids

Do you ever get fed up with being treated like a kid? Want to be treated like a grown-up? Not if you were a Victorian kid you wouldn't. Because Victorian children could be *punished* like adults! One boy told his story to a reporter…

THE BEGGAR'S TALE

Our reporter met a boy of about ten as he left prison and the boy told his story. We present it here for our readers. Judge for yourselves the state of Queen Victoria's Britain.

I was born in Wisbech near Cambridge. My mother died when I was five and my father married again. My stepmother hated me so I ran away.

I lived by begging and sleeping rough and made my way to London. There I'd sleep on doorsteps or anywhere that gave a little shelter. I suffered terribly from hunger and at times I thought I'd starve. I got crusts but I can hardly tell how I lived.

One night I was sleeping under a railway bridge when a policeman came along and asked me what I was up to. I told him I had no place to go and he said I had to go with him.

The next morning he took me to court and told the judge there were always a lot of boys living under the bridge. They

> were young thieves and they gave a lot of trouble. I was mixing with them so I was given 14 days in prison.
>
> I'll carry on begging and go from workhouse to workhouse to sleep. I am unhappy but I have to get used to it.

We don't know what happened to this boy. Did he ever find happiness? Did anyone care?

Some boys went pick-pocketing and were not bothered if they were caught. If they were sent to prison then at least they had food and shelter.

Child cheats

Want to make some dishonest money? Of course you don't. But if you DID, here are some tips from villainous Victorian children you must NOT try at home…

The shivering dodge

ON A COLD MORNING DRESS IN YOUR THINNEST CLOTHES AND STAND ON A STREET CORNER. START SHIVERING AND PLEADING FOR MONEY, TO BUY A WARM COAT. TAKE A WORN HANDKERCHIEF AND COUGH INTO IT AS IF YOU ARE ILL

I'M PERISHING

GET LOST, YOU LITTLE PERISHER!

The shivering dodge was a favourite of 'Shaking Jemmy'. He went on shivering so long he couldn't stop himself – even when he was in a warm house.

The lucifer dodge

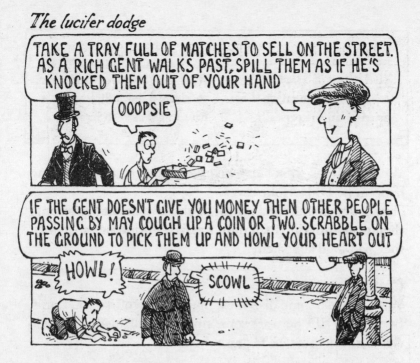

You can get your little friends to gather up the matches and try it again ... and again...

The tea and sugar dodge

This dodge could earn up to 18 shillings in one morning when many working men didn't make ten shillings a week.

The scaldrum dodge

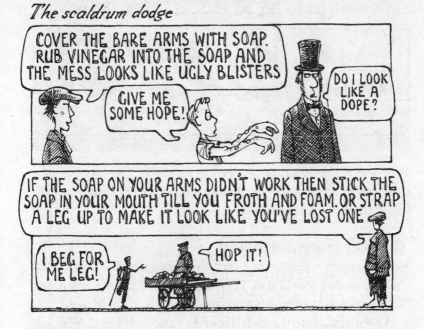

If looking ill doesn't help then pretend to choke on a piece of dry bread. Take money to get ale to wash the dry bread from your throat.

If everything fails then try this really disgusting one...

The bird-bread dodge

It is best if the bread is covered in maggots. Do NOT shake them off before you eat the bread – after all, they make a nice bit of meat in your sandwich.

Terrible transportation

Really serious villains were sent to America in the 1600s. But the Americans rebelled in 1776 and refused to take any more Brit criminals – after all, they had enough of their own.

About the same time as America rebelled, Captain Cook discovered Australia. A big, almost-empty place for dumping British villains. They were usually sent for 7, 10 or 14 years to suffer hard labour.

Imagine that! Sent away from your damp slum houses, your dreadful diseases, your smelly streets and your putrid water to the horrible sun and fresh air of Australia. Ugh!

The journey was a punishment in itself, though. It took four or five months in a rickety sailing ship. Out of every 100 prisoners transported one would die before they even got to Australia.

This 'transportation' to Australia lasted until the 1850s.

How bad did you have to be to be transported? It depended where you lived.

- In Yorkshire you were transported if it was your *third* crime.
- In Warwickshire and Dublin you were transported if it was your *second* crime.
- In Leeds and Manchester you could go to Australia for your *first* crime.

And age didn't matter too much. Children weren't supposed to be transported till they were 14 but younger ones were sent early in Victoria's reign...

Which of these crimes would get a child sent to Australia for seven years in the 1840s?

Stealing two loaves of bread from a baker – 11-year-old, Cheltenham

Spitting on the pavement – 13-year-old, Bath

Stealing three spoons – 11-year-old, Dublin

Stealing money – 8-year-old, London

Skiving off school – 10-year-old, Aberdeen

Answer: 1, 3 and 4 got children under 14 sent to Australia. It was theft that was taken really seriously by the judges. In 1849 Michael Walton was transported for ten years for stealing two turkeys and ten hens – that's almost a year for each bird!

Terrible transportation facts

1 Girls were hardly ever transported. Out of every eight convicts transported only one was a woman.

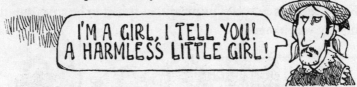

2 Young villains were taught in a school on the ship. Who was the schoolmaster? A convict, of course.

3 Transportation schools taught about an hour of English and an hour of maths each day. At the end of the week there was always a test.

4 The most terrible transportation? Probably a boy sent to Australia at the age of six. It was said he could hardly talk properly.

5 Transported villains could be punished AGAIN if they did wrong in Australia. A transported boy of 16 grew to hate his prison officer so much that he attacked him with an axe. The officer's leg was so badly injured that it had to be amputated. The boy was hanged.

Horrible hulks

When the prisons filled up, the courts had to send criminals to 'hulks'. These were old ships that were too ancient and rotten to sail. They were left in the river to rot and were filled with prisoners. They were crowded, damp and full of rats.

There was even a 'hulk' for young criminals – the *Euryalus*. The work was boring, and the kids kept themselves amused by bullying. The only escape was to fall sick and get on to the hospital hulk, the *Wye*.

How do you get on to a hospital ship? Don't try this at home...

Sometimes a friend would help you break your arm. They'd hold your arm on a bench, then let a dinner table fall on it. Ouch!

Miserable mother

A child was taken to court in Birmingham. He was a thief. The judge said to the child's mother...

IF I SET THE BOY FREE, WILL YOU TAKE HIM HOME AND MAKE SURE HE BEHAVES?

CERTAINLY NOT!

Would *your* mother rather see you in prison than take you home? (Better not ask her in case she says 'yes'.)

The judge had to send the boy to a hulk. The boy was too feeble to take it, and died. He was six years and seven months old. A young Victorian villain who got what he deserved? Villainous Victorian victim.

Little devils

In 1857 a new law was passed and it came up with a new way of punishing little criminals who committed little crimes. What was this new punishment?

a) Little devils were whipped ten times with a leather belt.

b) Little devils were sent to school.

c) Little devils were fastened in stocks and pelted with cold cabbage.

CUT OFF MY FINGERS? PHEW! FOR A MINUTE THERE I THOUGHT YOU WERE GOING TO SEND ME TO SCHOOL

d) Little devils were fastened in stocks and pelted with hot cabbage.

e) Little devils had their little fingers cut off.

Answer: b) 'That's right – as *a punishment* children were sent to school.

The Industrial Schools Act of 1857 let judges send children from 7 to 14 to 'industrial schools' where they would be taught reading and writing, and learn useful skills like sewing and woodwork.

In 1861 the law said the industrial schools should be used for any child...

- under 14 caught begging;
- found wandering homeless;
- found with a gang of thieves;
- under 12 who has committed a crime;
- under 14 whose parents say they are out of control.

See that last one? That's probably why YOU'VE been sentenced to school.

YOU CAN SEE FOR YOURSELF, OFFICER, SHE'S COMPLETELY OUT OF CONTROL

And industrial schools were even worse than the ones you have to go to. Children worked from six in the morning till seven at night.

You'd be too *tired* to go 'out of control' after that.

Trouble with trousers

What would *you* do if you were a Victorian judge? Here is a true case from Scotland. There is no doubt that the girl is guilty. She admits it. If you set her free, then the posh people of the town will have you sacked – they don't want thieves to get away with their crimes. (After all, those rich people could be next.) But how much punishment do you give this villainous Victorian girl?

BOWMORE COURT
ISLE OF ISLAY – SCOTLAND

ACCUSED: *Margaret Cowan*

AGE: *About 11 years old*

ADDRESS: *The Poor House, Islay.*

DATE: *13 February 1857*

CRIME: *Stealing a pair of trousers. She exchanged the trousers for two biscuits, which she then ate.*

RECORD: *Has already been found guilty of stealing a pair of shoes. She exchanged these for some porridge, which she ate.*

PUNISHMENT:

Well, judge? You can send her to prison, send her to prison *with* hard labour, send her for transportation to Australia, or send her to a reform school, where she will learn useful work.

Answer: Margaret was sent to prison in Argyll for 40 days *and* then she was sent to reform school in Glasgow for three years. Pretty harsh for stealing a pair of trousers worth a couple of biscuits.

As Margaret Cowan didn't say…

THAT IS PANTS

It wasn't just Scotland that was tough on little villains. In 1875 Emily Davies (aged 13) was caught pinching apples from a rich man's garden in Ross-on-Wye (on the border between England and Wales). Like Margaret Cowan, she got prison followed by *four* years in reform school.

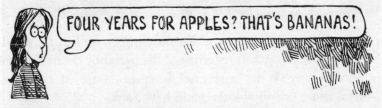

FOUR YEARS FOR APPLES? THAT'S BANANAS!

Emily wept as she was led off to prison. But there was good news for her. Her case caused so much protest that she was set free after a few weeks.

Did you know…?

For being cheeky to his prison teacher James Richmond was locked in a dungeon with only wooden planks to sleep on and bread and water for two days. Punishments like this, time after time, made him ill and he died in prison. James Richmond was just ten years old.

Crime school

In 1870 a new law said there had to be schools for everyone. This took criminal kids off the streets and into criminal classrooms instead.

The kids learned maths and English and so on but they did *not* learn speaking and listening skills like they do in British schools today. What a shame! Imagine some of the *true* stories those criminal kids could have told...

This happened in London in 1848 but could have happened almost any time, any place, in Victoria's Britain.

MY DAD CAME HOME DRUNK ONE NIGHT AND SAID HE WAS GOING TO DROWN ME AND MY BROTHER. HE TOLD OUR STEP-MOTHER TO FETCH OUR SHOES. SHE JUST SAID, 'IF YOU'RE GOING TO DROWN THEM YOU MAY AS WELL LEAVE THE SHOES FOR ME TO SELL.' HE TOOK US AND THREW ME IN. I WAS ONLY SAVED BY A BOATMAN THAT FISHED ME OUT

In 1852 this really happened. Many parents dropped unwanted babies into canals in Victorian times, but it was not so common for them to try to kill off grown boys!

SHOPKEEPER

ME AND MY FRIENDS START A FIGHT OUTSIDE A SHOP AND MAYBE BUMP AGAINST THE WINDOW. WHEN THE SHOPKEEPER COMES OUT TO SORT US OUT, ONE OF THE LADS NIPS IN AND ROBS HIS TILL

Children as young as six years old were up to this trick. Sometimes they used girls to get the shopkeeper's mind off his till by talking to him. They thought shopkeepers would trust girls more than boys. Hmm.

The boy was eight years old when, in 1855, he was flogged and locked in prison for stealing a few plums.

Did you know…?
There's a game that has been played ever since doors were invented. But in the 1850s it was against the law and children who were caught could go to prison…

Young people could also be locked up for throwing stones – sometimes they threw them at gas-lamps in the street. One boy threw mud and was locked up.

Hanging around

Execution in Victorian Britain was by hanging. Up to the year 1868 convicted people were hanged in public – and crowds turned up to watch. They turned it into a bit of a holiday. One of the most famous executions of Victoria's time was of Mr Frederick and Mrs Maria Manning.

The Mannings had killed Patrick O'Connor after inviting him round to their house for a meal. O'Connor was a rich moneylender and the cut-throat couple planned to rob him.

First Maria shot O'Connor and then husband Frederick beat him to finish him off. Frederick told the judge…

I NEVER LIKED HIM MUCH

Thank you, Frederick, I think we might have guessed that.

The terrible twosome buried O'Connor under their kitchen floor but were found out and sentenced to hang.

A public execution was also a chance for pickpockets to work in the crowds. One thief described the fun he had at the Mannings' hanging…

Mrs Manning was dressed beautiful when she came up. She screeched when the hangman pulled the bolt away. I made four shillings and sixpence at the hanging – I nicked two handkerchiefs and a purse with two shillings in it. It was the best purse I ever had.

Mrs Manning was 'dressed beautiful' in a black satin dress. After the hanging those dresses suddenly went out of fashion. Wonder why?

As usual, reports of the murder and the hanging sold thousands of copies at a penny a time. These reports were called 'broadsides' and some of them were written in verse…

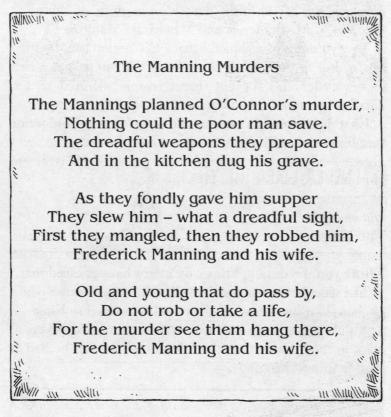

The Manning Murders

The Mannings planned O'Connor's murder,
Nothing could the poor man save.
The dreadful weapons they prepared
And in the kitchen dug his grave.

As they fondly gave him supper
They slew him – what a dreadful sight,
First they mangled, then they robbed him,
Frederick Manning and his wife.

Old and young that do pass by,
Do not rob or take a life,
For the murder see them hang there,
Frederick Manning and his wife.

Models of the Mannings appeared in Madame Tussaud's waxwork museum in London. Visitors went along and threw coins at the wax dummies – though that probably didn't hurt as much as the hanging.

A reporter sneered…

George Manning is greatly improved by his appearance in Madame Tussaud's. He looks like a very clean undertaker.

That's a bit unkind to undertakers, who are very nice people!

Charles Dickens was at the Manning execution and wrote about it with horror. It gave him nightmares – and he was a grown man. Dickens changed Mrs Manning's name to Hortense and put her into his book *Bleak House*.

Did you know…?

The Victorians may have been ruthless when it came to hanging people. But they were better than 30 years before. Before Victoria came to the throne, they hanged children.

- In 1800 a boy of ten was hanged. The judge said…

WE DON'T WANT CHILDREN THINKING THEY CAN GET AWAY WITH CRIMES

- In 1801 a boy of 13 was hanged for breaking into a house and stealing a spoon.

- In 1808 two sisters were hanged in Lynn for theft. One was aged 11. Her little sister was just eight.
- In 1831, just six years before Victoria took the throne, a nine-year-old boy was hanged at Chelmsford for setting fire to a house.

Anyone under seven was too young to be hanged. The problem was there were no birth certificates to prove your age until 1837. So how did you know if a person was too young to hang?

Scaffold school

But what about the children who went along to an execution? If adults were sickened by the horror of hanging then surely parents wouldn't take their children along to an execution?

But many did. After all, it was a lesson...

The last man to suffer hanging in public was Michael Barrett. What might a child have made of the day of his death...

It was a picnic. Thousands of men, women and children stood in the square outside Newgate Prison. They chattered and laughed, and tucked into their breakfasts. A few hundred of the richer ones sat at the upstairs windows of the houses opposite the prison. They paid good money for the view.

Outside the prison wall stood a wooden platform. There was a scaffold above it with a dangling noose and in the floor was a trapdoor with a bolt.

As eight o'clock struck on the prison clock the babble of noise dropped to a murmur. The prisoner, Michael Barrett, was led out of the prison, his hands tied.

'What are they doing with that man?' a child's voice piped through the quiet morning air.

'They're going to hang him by the neck till he's dead,' his mother murmured.

'Why are they doing that?' the child asked.

'Because he's wicked. He killed twenty people!' the woman hissed.

A gentleman beside her said, 'It was twelve people dead and about a hundred injured.'

'Twelve, then,' the woman sniffed.

'Did he shoot them?' the child asked and had pictures in his head of a dozen loaded guns.

'No, my child,' the man sighed. 'The man on the platform is Michael Barrett – an Irishman. His friends were locked away in Clerkenwell Prison and he tried to get them out.'

'How did he do that?' the child persisted.

'He took a barrel of gunpowder and put it up against the prison wall. He thought his friends were on the other side of the wall and, when it was blown down, they'd be able to escape.'

'And did they get away?' the child gasped, her round eyes blinking.

'No. The prison officers knew something was going to happen so they locked the prisoners away. The blast blew down the wall but it also wrecked a lot of houses in the street called Corporation Row nearby. A lot of people died.'

The child turned pale and looked back towards the wooden platform. The prisoner in his dark red coat and striped grey trousers was climbing to the top of the platform with a steady tread, and talking to the priest who was waiting there.

Then the door in the prison wall opened again and the crowd gasped with horror. A powerful old man with a grey beard stepped out. He wore a tight black cap and a dark cloak. He was the grimmest and ugliest man the child had ever seen. She shrank behind her mother's skirts.

'That's William Calcraft – the executioner,' the man explained. 'A butcher. His victims always die a slow and painful death. I don't know why they keep him in the job.'

'Because no one else would do it,' the woman said. She was pushed in the back as the crowd jostled and surged towards the platform to get a better look. The child was so tight against her mother's skirt that she couldn't see what was happening at the scaffold.

The girl turned to the man. 'Lift me up!' she pleaded.

'No,' he said. He took a fountain pen and a notebook from his pocket and began to scribble words.

He glanced up and saw the executioner disappear beneath the scaffold. A hush fell on the vast crowd so great that the child could hear sparrows fighting on the rooftops and the scratch of the man's pen. There was a grating sound as the bolt of the trapdoor was pulled.

There was a gasp from the crowd, then a roar and a half-hearted cheer. 'That's what the Fenians deserve!' a man cried.

'She's fainted,' a woman groaned and the girl turned to see a young woman being carried out of the tightly packed crowd.

'That's Michael Barrett's girlfriend ... poor girl,' the man sighed and scribbled some more.

'I couldn't see anything,' the girl sighed as the crowd turned away and began to thin.

The man put his pen and notebook back in his pocket. 'And you never will,' he said to the girl.

'What do you mean?'

The man tugged his dark beard. 'I mean this will stop soon ... hanging men in public will stop. It's barbaric. Something from the Middle Ages. The public have no right to see it – children should not be allowed to see it.'

The girl's mother turned an angry shade of red. 'Teach the child a lesson. That's what happens to killers.'

The man shook his head. 'The people here today didn't come to learn a lesson. They came to see an innocent man murdered with a rope.'

'Innocent?' the woman jeered. 'What do you know? A jury found him guilty. Who are you to say he didn't do it? Eh?'

The girl had never heard her mother so angry. The woman waved a finger in the man's face.

'Eh? Go on. Tell me. Who are you?' she ranted.

The man raised his hat politely and said quietly. 'My name is Dickens, madam. Charles Dickens. You may have heard of me.'

He patted the girl on the head and turned away from the mother whose mouth hung open foolishly.

'Can we go and look at the dead man now, Mum?' the girl asked.

The mother wrapped a shawl around the child's head and dragged her off down the street. 'No, child. No. Let's go home.'

Michael Barrett was a Fenian. The Fenians were Irish people who didn't want English Queen Victoria ruling them. They tried to drive the British out with bombs and killings. In 1881 the Fenians tried to blow up Salford Army Camp but only managed to kill a seven-year-old boy. The Fenians were dangerous but not very successful.

(There were eight attempts to kill Queen Victoria in 60 years – four of those were Irish attempts. In 1887 Victoria went to Parliament to celebrate her 50 years as queen. There was a Fenian plot, just like Guy Fawkes's, to blow her up with her ministers. Several ministers knew about it and were sure they could stop the attack. They did, but they let Vic take the risk anyway!)

Barrett said at his trial:

I have never deliberately injured a human being. I love my country and if it would help Ireland, I would willingly sacrifice my life – I will meet death without a murmur.

Many people believed him when he said he hurt no one. They said the police bribed and bullied people to say they saw Barrett at the scene of the Clerkenwell explosion. Barrett had to die to make it look as if Victoria's police were doing their job.

Many years after Barrett's death, another Fenian admitted that he planted the bomb that exploded at Clerkenwell. Barrett was innocent. So the police were suspected of telling porkies.

Charles Dickens was so sickened by public hangings that he was one of the people who spoke out against them and had them stopped. Three days after Michael Barrett was executed the law was changed so no one was ever hanged in public again.

Terrible timeline 1850s-1860s

Famous and Fortunate   *Forgotten and Failed*

1853

Dr **John Snow** was born in 1813 in a York slum. One of the first doctors to use 'chloroform' to knock patients out before he saws off bits of their body or sticks a surgeon's knife into them. Dr J uses chloroform on Queen Vic so she can have a baby (Prince Leopold) with no pain. Vic likes it and makes slum-kid Snow rich ... till he dies this year aged just 45.

Thady Wynne and brother Michael kill a man and are sentenced to being 'transported' to Australia. Michael is too poorly to travel but Thady leaves his wife and seven children back in Curreentorpan. He should be famous as one of the LAST ever convicts to be sent to Australia – the Australians don't want any more! But Thady is forgotten.

I KNOCKED OUT THE QUEEN, DRUGGED PEOPLE, CUT THEM UP AND CHOPPED OFF ARMS AND LEGS

SO HOW COME YOU'RE NOT BEING SENT TO AUSTRALIA?

1854

Florence Nightingale – a posh kid who hears God calling her to do something good – leads a team of nurses to help the sick Brit soldiers dying of disease in the Crimean War in 1854. (She is

Mortimer Grimshaw is a leader of the Preston Cotton Mill workers' strike. They don't want a pay rise – they just want back the money the bosses have cut. The bosses close the factories and

really clever at maths and it helps her do sums that will save lives.) Becomes ill and blind for so long she takes more nursing than she gave out! Sickly Flo doesn't enjoy her fame much.

try to starve the workers till they are forced to go back to work. The workers give in. So Mort Grim is a failure – though 12 years before, five Preston strikers were shot dead. So Mort was a lucky failure.

1857

David **Livingstone**, the Scottish explorer, comes back from exploring Africa a hero! He has discovered vast waterfalls and named them after Victoria – the creep! He has also shown the way for Brits to get into Africa – they will take diseases and Christianity in, and they will take wealth out. But Dave's a hero, so that's all right.

In India British troops are taking over from leaders like **Nana Sahib**. Nana leads the Indian Mutiny and holds Brit women and children prisoners. When the British attack him at Lucknow he has 200 of them hacked to pieces and the bits thrown down a well. Doesn't do him much good. Brits win – Nana vanishes and probably dies.

1865

Edward J Eyre is the governor of Jamaica when the Jamaicans rebel against Brit rule. Evil Edward had rebels shot, hanged, and even had heads hacked off and stuck on poles like a ruler from the Middle Ages. He is brought back to Britain, where a lot of people think he did a good job. He is not punished for the 400 men and women he had massacred. A nice way to get famous!

Edward Whymper is one of a group of four Brits to get to the top of the Matterhorn mountain in Switzerland. But only Ed came back. The others fell 1,400 metres off the mountain on to a glacier below – very careless that, and rather painful. Whymper gets home; yet it is the famous (but splattered) leader Lord Francis Douglas who is remembered. Whymper's no wimp but he is forgotten.

Massacre man   Matterhorn man

1867

Alfred Nobel, the Swedish inventor, shows off his new invention in Surrey. It is a high explosive called 'dynamite'. It will kill millions over the years. It will make a really good weapon for rebels! But Alf will give money for 'Peace prizes' – so he'll be remembered as a man of peace

Charles Brett is a poor policeman who's in the wrong place. The Irish are revolting. The leaders of the rebel group, the Fenians, are arrested. Their friends hold up the police van and order Sergeant Brett to open the door. But Brett refuses. He puts his eye to the keyhole

even though he made himself rich and famous with something so deadly. Funny old world.

to see what's happening – just as a Fenian puts a bullet through the keyhole. Ouch!

1869

Dr **Joseph Lister** operates on sick people using disinfectant and only 15 per cent of his patients die from his operation – with other doctors it's 45 per cent. He has a nasty habit of doing tests by cutting up live animals. Queen Vic tries to stop him but she fails. Cat-cutting, rabbit-ripping Dr L goes on to fame and fortune. Animals are not amused. Lister later operates on Vic and she makes him 'Sir Joseph'.

Mrs **Josephine Butler** sets up ... deep breath ... 'The Ladies Association for the Repeal of the Contagious Diseases Acts'. The laws say homeless girls can be injected by police doctors whether they have diseases or not. ('Police wouldn't dare do it to me,' Mrs Butler reckons.) She wins – in 1886, after 17 years! So, not a failure, but almost forgotten – after all those years of struggle.

Mr Peel's pained police

Sir Robert Peel thought the nightwatchmen in London were pretty useless at stopping the villains. So he created the police force in 1829. When Victoria came to the throne police forces began to spread all over Britain – like spots on a kid with chicken pox.

They popped up everywhere. You may think people would be glad to have their local police there to protect them. But at first they weren't all that popular.

Here are 10 foul facts…

1. They call us nasty names

It's not very nice being called names, is it? Your teacher would *hate* to be called 'fat face' just because she has a fat face, wouldn't she? Well policemen hated the cruel names the public called them. Victoria's police were called names like…

- **Peelers** – No, NOT potato peelers. They were named after Robert Peel who invented them.
- **Peel's Bloody Gang** – Charming.
- **Raw Lobsters** – Not because there was something fishy about them, but because raw lobsters are blue and so is a policeman's uniform.
- **Blue Devils** – not to be confused with Manchester United FC who are nicknamed the Red Devils.
- **Crushers** – Well they could give your head a bit of a crushing with those truncheons.

- **Cheese** – But dairy you call a policeman that today?
- **Cops (or Coppers)** – The Romans used the word *capere*, which means to capture. That's what policemen did so they became 'caps' and then the word changed to 'cops'. Bet your history teacher didn't know that!
- **Pigs** – Some things never change.
- **Rozzers** – A word meaning 'strong man' in gypsy language (used from about 1890).
- **Noses** – Because the police stick their noses into villains' business? Who nose?
- **Slops** – Because 's-l-o-p' is 'police' spelt backwards. Almost.

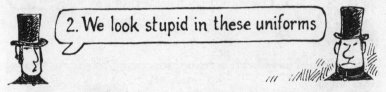

2. We look stupid in these uniforms

PC Cavanagh described how he was dressed on his first day:

When I looked at myself in the mirror I wondered why on earth I had decided to become a peeler. My top hat was slipping all over my head, my boots were two sizes too large and were rubbing the skin off my heels; my thick leather neck tie was almost choking me. I would have given all I owned to get back into ordinary clothes!

Of course, the leather neck tie was to keep away garrotters.

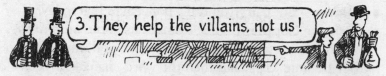

3. They help the villains, not us!

The law said you had to help a policeman if he needed it. If you refused, then you could go to jail. But the ordinary people often helped criminals by warning them. As soon as they saw a policeman in the north of England, the cry was: 'Cheese, my lads!'

In London children chanted...

I spy blue, I spy black! I spy a peeler in a shiny hat!

(They should have been arrested for trying to rhyme 'black' and 'hat'.)

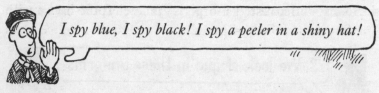

4. They lie to us

Some children were taught by their parents to lie to the police. A man was accused of being drunk. His little daughter told the police...

He couldn't have been drinking that afternoon. He was having a shave from 1 p.m. till 6 p.m.

They arrested the man anyway. The judge didn't believe the girl for some reason.

London Police Inspector Restiaux was lucky to escape with his life in November 1840. He led a group of policemen into the slums and arrested a forger. As they left the house with the forger a crowd gathered and pelted the police with stones.

The police fled with their prisoner but the mob charged. The mob leader had a knife. Restiaux wrestled with him and disarmed the man. The police escaped with the forger to the safety of the police station.

The slums were known as 'The Holy Land' – Restiaux could have ended up with a holey hand.

The rich people were forced to pay the taxes that paid for police wages. Earl Waldegrave had a real hatred of the police. Once Waldegrave paid a professional boxer to attack PC McKenzie in Piccadilly, London, while crowds of his friends watched. The boxer almost killed the policeman.

The rich sometimes told their coachmen to lash out at policemen in the streets as they drove past. Some even drove their coaches straight *at* the police.

Earl Waldegrave and a friend jumped on PC Wheatley and held him on the ground while his coach drove over him. PC Wheatley lived, but was badly hurt.

He never worked again.

Policemen worked 10 hours a day and walked about 20 miles on duty. Nearly a marathon every day. They had no days off and only one week's holiday a year ... and they didn't get paid when they were on holiday.

Birmingham had no police force in 1839. That year riots started there and the government sent for the London police.

A hundred police eventually calmed the troubles. Then 60 policemen were sent back to London – and the rioters heard that only 40 were left in Birmingham. The rioters drove the

40 police into a yard and trapped them there while they ran through the town, burning and stealing. The army had to be sent in to free the police.

10. And sometimes the job is disgusting

The police went to the worst slums to arrest criminals. And criminals could have some very dirty habits. One policeman reported...

I entered the house and began to search it. I thought the gang had used the cupboard as a hiding place for stolen goods. I found the gang had been using the cupboard as a toilet.

Another policeman reported...

I found a wellington boot on the seashore ... with a man's foot inside it.

A POLICEMAN'S LIFE IS *NOT* A HAPPY ONE!

YOU SAID IT, MATE

Awful arrests

The police sometimes had to arrest people for the saddest of crimes. For example, in Victorian times there were often cases where women killed their own babies. In 1846, in a Durham village, Margaret Stoker drowned her 14-month-old daughter. She was so desperately poor that she couldn't bear to see the baby starve slowly to death.

The policeman told his story...

Margaret Stoker was sentenced to death but the judge took pity on her and let her live.

Pickpocket police

The 'dredger-men' didn't trust the police at all. Who were these 'dredger-men'? Well, they had one of the most cheerful and charming jobs in Victorian England – they went out on the river and fished out dead bodies.

They helped to keep the river clean and were paid for every body they found. But they could also rob the corpses before they handed them over.

A reporter who wrote about London said:

> *It is strange that no body brought in by a dredger-man ever happens to have any money about it when it is brought to shore. And the dredgers do not see anything dishonest about emptying the pockets of a dead man. They say that anyone who finds a body would do the same. And if they didn't do it then the police would!*

Foul feuds

Big Victorian cities were filled with 'costers' – people who sold food or clothes or goods from barrows in the streets. (It was cheaper to buy a barrow than to buy a shop.) But the barrows could clutter up the streets and the police often removed them. Sometimes a coster thought a policeman had it in for him and plotted his revenge.

A writer called Mayhew described what happened in one case...

> The costers believe that getting revenge on a policeman is one of the bravest things a young man can do. Some men went to prison time after time for attacking the police and the costers treated them like heroes.
>
> Sometimes a coster would track an enemy policeman for months till he got a chance to attack him. One young man I spoke to waited six months for his revenge. He told me, proudly, that he rushed in and gave the policeman a savage kicking. 'When I heard he was injured for life, I was full of joy. They sent me to prison for a year but, believe me, it was worth it.'

These costers were often violent people who lived in a violent world of their own and they gave themselves odd nicknames. One woman was called 'Cast Iron Polly' because she was hit over the head with a cast-iron pan once and it didn't hurt her.

SEE? NO EFFECT. JUST HER OLD, NORMAL SELF

THAT'S NORMAL?

Here are ten coster nicknames – two have been made up ... can you spot which two are the odd ones out?

Wicked for women

Women had a rotten time in Victoria's Britain. Husbands were allowed to beat their wives with sticks … so long as the stick was no thicker than his thumb. And even if a young man was just a 'boyfriend' he treated a girl as if he owned her. One 16-year-old boy put it this way…

> *If I seed my gal talking to another chap I'd give her such a punch of the nose it would sharp put a stop to it.*

> *HORRIBLE HISTORIES* HINT TO BULLIES: Notice he doesn't hit the 'chap'. Maybe because the 'chap' would hit him back? Remember – if you want to be a bully, be a coward first.

Some men even had the nerve to say…

> *It's an odd thing but the girls axully like a feller for walloping them. As long as the bruises hurt she'll be thinking of the bloke that gave them to her.*

Sounds like a good excuse for the school bully, doesn't it? 'Actually, sir, the wimps love it when I hit them … so that's all right, isn't it?'

And if the boyfriends didn't beat the young women then their parents could do it instead. Some girls were sent out to sell things like apples. If they came back with the apples instead of the money, there was trouble…

There's many a girl I know whose back gets lashed if she doesn't sell enough.

PLEASE

Anyway, you can see why Victorian women grew up tough. And some grew up wicked. Take Elizabeth Pearson, for example…

Busy Lizzie

Elizabeth Pearson was 28 years old in 1875. She lived with her husband and son in Gainford, County Durham. Her uncle and aunt lived nearby and then her aunt died…

NEVER MIND, UNCLE JIM. I'LL TAKE CARE OF YOU

I'LL TAKE CARE OF HIM ONCE AND FOR ALL

The jury did not say, 'Show her mercy'. So she was sent to hang at Durham Prison.

At 8 a.m. on the morning of 2 August 1875 Elizabeth Pearson was taken to the gallows with two other killers, both men. All three were to hang together. Elizabeth Pearson was the calmest of the three.

Her husband and son wept, but no one else did. At 8:03 a.m. a black flag was raised over the prison to show the executions had been completed. Villainous Victorian.

Battered Bridget

The day before Elizabeth Pearson was arrested a man called John Tully was arrested just 35 miles away in Hartlepool. He was charged with killing his wife, Bridget.

Witnesses said John Tully kicked his wife in the stomach, held her tight by the hair to beat her and smashed her against the wall. He was caught when he was just about to hit her with a poker.

Tully was found guilty of beating his wife. Remember, Elizabeth Pearson had hanged for murdering her uncle. What happened to John Tully for his actions?

a) He was one of the men hanged alongside Elizabeth Pearson.

b) He was sent to prison for 20 years because the killing was accidental.

c) He was sent to prison for nine months.

So what's the message? A woman kills a man – she hangs. A man kills a woman – he goes to prison for nine months. Is that fair? Maybe not, but that's Victorian justice for you.

Pretty deadly

If Victorian Britain was tough for women, then some fought back with any weapon they could get hold of. The idea of a killer woman made a good story, and three cases in particular hit the headlines. Here are four casebooks – three really happened and one of them was invented for a novel. But can you tell which is the made-up one and which three are true?

Murdering Maddie

Name: Madeleine Smith
Aged 21 in 1857. Living in Glasgow.

Victim: Her boyfriend, Pierre Emile L'Angelier
Madeleine's mum and dad didn't like Emile and found her a better husband. Emile was furious and said he'd show the world the love letters she had written to him. They said mushy things like...

> 3 September 1855
> I live for you alone; I adore you. I could never love another as I do you. Oh dearest Emile, I wish I could clasp you to me heart right now.

The letters would wreck her marriage. Emile had to go.

Method: Poisoned by arsenic
Madeleine had bought arsenic poison at chemist shops. She said it was to put on her skin to make her look good. Emile died with at least 14 grams of arsenic inside him – enough to give an elephant gut ache.

L'Angelier

What happened? The court said 'Not Proven'. That's Scottish Law meaning, 'We know you did it but we can't prove it.' The problem was she bought the poison, he had it inside him, but no one could prove that she actually gave it to him. Madeleine went free. Villainous Victorian? Probably.

Awful Aurora

Name: Aurora Floyd
Aged 27 in 1862. Living near Doncaster.

Victim: Her ex-husband, James Conyers
Aurora married Conyers but left him because he beat her and went off with other women. She read a report that he had been killed so she thought she was free to marry John Mellish and she did. Conyers turned up and threatened to tell her new husband she was already married.

Darling Aurora,
 I cannot tell you how surprised I was to hear you had married another man. As I remember, you are still married to me. But do not worry, I can keep my mouth shut. For a price.
Meet me one week from tonight by the pool in the forest and bring £2,000. That is how much my silence will cost.
        Your loving husband (still!) JC

Conyers had to go.

Method: Shot in the back
The corpse of Conyers was found near a pool in the forest. When the police looked at his clothes they found a marriage certificate proving Aurora Floyd was married to the dead man. She was questioned and told them she

had met her ex-husband in the wood and had paid him £2000 to go away. She said she had not killed him – but there was no money on the corpse.

What happened? Aurora Floyd was released without charge. A servant was later blamed for shooting Conyers and stealing the £2,000. Villainous Victorian? Not really.

Flighty Florrie

Name: Florence Bravo
Aged 30 in 1876. Living in Balham, London.

Victim: Her husband, Charles Bravo
Florence was a good 'friend' of an old doctor called James Gully but Dr James was already married. So she married Charles Bravo. Charles turned out to be a bully and a meanie. He grew worse when a mystery writer sent him a letter...

MR BRAVO
YOUR WIFE LOVES DR JAMES GULLY. NOT YOU. YOU ONLY MARRIED HER FOR HER MONEY SO YOU DESERVE IT.
                    SIGNED,   A FRIEND

Bully Bravo had to go.

Method: Poisoned by antimony
This poison was used in the Bravo stables to kill stomach worms in horses. It has no taste. Charles Bravo drank wine at dinner and was taken ill. He died three days later.

What happened? The court said he had been murdered – but they couldn't say who did it. Florence went free – but drank herself to death two years later. Villainous Victorian? Probably.

Foul Flo

Name: Florence Maybrick
American, living in Liverpool, 1889.

Victim: Her husband, James Maybrick
James was 24 years older than Florence. Florence had a boyfriend in Liverpool but James was no angel – he had several girlfriends himself. He was also a drug addict. James had to go.

Method: Poisoned by arsenic
Arsenic was found in meat juice. Florence had bought fly-papers and soaked them to get the arsenic out of them. She said it was for her skin. But ... James was found dead with arsenic in his body. The evidence made her look guilty but no one could decide how James had died.
• Some doctors said James died of a stomach fever.
• James was always sick and took lots of poisonous stuff to try to cure himself – including arsenic.

- James's family didn't like her or trust her. When he fell ill, they banned her from his sick room.
- No one could say how the arsenic got into James – did he take it himself? Did Florence feed him it in the meat juice? Did his family feed it to him AFTER they banned her from his room?

The judge was mentally ill and he told the jury...

Florence Maybrick had a good reason to want her husband dead

What happened? Florence was found guilty and sentenced to hang. The court <u>should</u> have set Florence free. Under pressure, the government said she had only 'tried' to kill her husband, and spared her life. She served 15 years in prison. Villainous Victorian? Maybe.

So which one was *not* a true case?

Answer: It was Awful Aurora. This was the plot of the novel *Aurora Floyd* written by Mary Elizabeth Braddon. It was a huge Victorian success, especially with women readers, and it was turned into a very popular play.

Foul fun

The Victorians didn't have television. So no soaps for them … in fact no *soap* for a lot of them either! But they did enjoy going to the theatre.

The Victorians enjoyed plays with a bit of blood and murder in them, and if they were based on a true story then they were even more popular. Top of the Victorian pops in plays was *Maria Marten – The Murder in the Red Barn*. It was the true story of Maria, who was murdered – guess where? Yes, in a red barn. Her boyfriend, William Corder, shot her and as she died she made a lovely speech…

William! I am dying! Your cruel hand has stilled the heart that beat in love for thee. Death claims me and, with my last breath, I die blessing and forgiving thee.

The crowds cheered for heroines like Maria, booed the villains like Corder and generally shouted at the actors – it was more like a football match today.

People peepers

Another way Victorians told stories was to put little puppets in a box. The viewers paid to peep through a hole and watch the puppets act out the story as one person told the tale and did all the voices. (This was cheaper than having a big stage with lots of actors, of course.)

The *Murder in the Red Barn* peep show was still popular in the 1860s, 30 years after the murder happened. It was so popular the box had to have 26 windows for people to peep.

In the 1860s a murder took place in the Red Lion pub in Berkshire, when a farm worker chopped the landlady with his reaping hook. One peep-show family group quickly changed the story of Maria Marten and added lots of red paint. What did they call the new play? *Murder in the Red Lion*, of course.

Petrifying plays

The Victorian audiences just loved villains – and they also loved amazing scenes. The following villains and amazing scenes were shown live on stage…

1 *Uncle Tom's Cabin*

Plot: Play based on the famous book about slavery in the USA.
Villain: Wicked slave owner.
Big scene: Slave girl Eliza escapes over frozen Ohio river, chased by dogs as a captured wild horse escapes.

2 *The Colleen Bawn*

Plot: An Irish story about a poor girl, Eily, with a posh husband who keeps her hidden.

Villain: Hardress Cregan – the husband

Big scene: Eily in a rowing boat with the murderous Danny, who pushes her in the lake. She is rescued by hero Myles.

3 *After Dark*

Plot: Play set in London and the Underground railway.

Villain: The criminal who drugs our hero.

Big scene: The hero is laid across the railway track and is rescued as a train rushes across the stage. The rescuer has broken through a cellar wall.

4 *The Octoroon*

Plot: A story about a slave girl (Zoë) in the USA (again).

Villain: The slave trader.

Big scene: A steamboat on the Mississippi river explodes, burns and sinks, killing Zoë.

THE GIRL STOOD ON THE BURNING DECK,
THE FIRE AROUND HER FLICKERS
A MIGHTY FLAME SHOOTS UP HER DRESS
AND SETS FIRE TO HER KNICKERS

5 *The Flying Scud*

Plot: A play about a racehorse that must win the Derby if the villains are to be defeated.

Villain: The bookmaker who drugs the jockey.

Big scene: A horse race with cardboard horses on a revolving stage – then a real horse enters at the end.

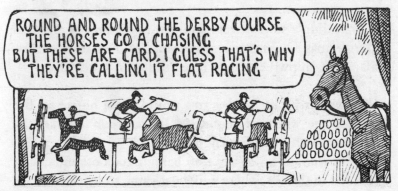

ROUND AND ROUND THE DERBY COURSE
THE HORSES GO A CHASING
BUT THESE ARE CARD, I GUESS THAT'S WHY
THEY'RE CALLING IT FLAT RACING

Did you know…?

A play called *The Derby Winner* tried to copy *The Flying Scud* and have a horse race on a turning stage. But the machine broke down on the first night. The actor had to stand in front of the curtains and say…

Putrid performances

In the pathetic play *Pluck* a train crashes. As the hero goes to rescue a trapped child from the wreckage, a second train crashes into it. The stage trains didn't look too good, and one newspaper said…

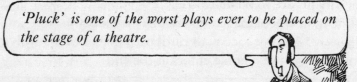

'Pluck' is one of the worst plays ever to be placed on the stage of a theatre.

But that didn't stop writers and actors making bigger and dafter dramas. On Victorian stages you could see earthquakes, avalanches, shipwrecks, boat races and even waterfalls.

- In *The Streets of London* you would see a house on fire across the width of the stage. It was then attacked by firemen with a real fire engine.
- In *The Ruling Passion* a hot-air balloon took off and crash-landed in the sea, where a lifeboat came to its rescue.

- In *The White Heather* the audience watched an underwater fight between the hero and villain dressed in diving suits. Each had a knife and the fight ended when the hero cut the villain's air-line and left him to drown. The stage appeared to be underwater and there even seemed to be fish swimming around the fighting men.

Why did these plays stop? Why can't you see them today? Because of a Victorian invention – the moving picture show. After 1920 the cinema was able to show bigger and more exciting scenes (using camera tricks) than they could ever do on stage. So in the end there was the most dramatic and sudden death of all – the death of the Victorian theatre.

Grim ghosts

Poor people couldn't afford to go to the theatre. So in the dim and flickering firelight of a gloomy evening, how did they entertain themselves? With stories.

And what better than a ghost story. Especially if it was a *true* ghost story. Here is a case from Cornwall about some villainous Victorians to chill your bones colder than a tombstone in the snow…

Listen, me dears, and I'll tell you the tale of two brothers. One brother was Edmund Norway and he was a seaman. On the night of 8th February 1840 he went to bed in his cabin and fell asleep around 11 p.m. He was a thousand miles away from his home in Cornwall.

He soon had a terrible dream that made him wake up sweating and screaming. He told it to the ship's officer, Henry Wren. He said...

'I dreamed I saw my brother killed. He was riding his horse along the road from Bodmin to Wadebridge. As he rode two men attacked him, and I watched in horror as one pointed a pistol at my brother. The pistol misfired twice so they dragged him from the horse and used the pistol to club him to death before they robbed him. Then one man dragged him across the road and dropped him in a ditch. I have a terrible fear that my brother has been murdered.'

Officer Wren said, 'It was just a bad dream. Go back to sleep. We'll be home in a week and you'll see your brother is safe and sound.'

But when Edmund Norway landed there was terrible news for him. 'Your brother, Nevell, has been murdered,' they said.

The constables had made an arrest. On 13th April William Lightfoot and his brother were found guilty of murdering Nevell Norway and sentenced to hang. Before he died, William confessed.

'I met my brother at the top of Dummer Hill and we plotted to rob the next person who came along. Around 11 p.m. we saw a man riding his horse along the road from Bodmin to Wadebridge. As he rode we two attacked him. He refused to hand over his money so I pointed my pistol at him. The pistol misfired twice so we dragged him from the horse and used the pistol to club him to death before we robbed him. Then my brother dragged him across the road and dropped him in a ditch.'

How did Edmund Norway know about his brother's death a thousand miles away and sailing in an ink-black sea?

Perhaps his brother's dying spirit slipped into his dreams to say farewell? Who knows? There's nothing as mysterious as death.

So, when the night time comes, and darkness falls, go gently, my dears, and may the angels watch over you.

Wrotten writers

The Victorians loved reading books. Popular writers then were like pop stars today – and just as wild and wacky in the way they lived.

Know-it-all adults think they know everything about Victorian writers. But you can find out just how much they know by asking them which of these odd facts about Victorian writers are true and which are false?

1 H G Wells had two pens for writing – a big pen for big words and a small pen for small words.
2 Charles Dickens' house was so cold his ink froze solid.

3 Poet Alfred Tennyson amused his friends by sitting down and pretending to be someone on a toilet.
4 Playwright Dion Boucicault said, 'On my gravestone I want you to write, "Not dead, just sleeping".'
5 Author Joseph Conrad tried to shoot himself ... but missed.
6 Playwright Oscar Wilde wrote *The Ballad of Reading Gaol* in jail.

7 Joseph Kipling wrote *The Jungle Book*.

8 Poet William Wordsworth wrote about flowers (like his famous 'Daffodils' poem) because he was mad about their smell.

9 Writer Anthony Trollope stood for Parliament and won.

10 Poet Algernon Swinburne ate his pet monkey for dinner.

Answers:

1 True. In his book *The History of Mr Polly* his character says, 'Sesquippledan verboojuice!' It means 'big words'. What sort of pen did he need for that?

2 False. Dickens was poor as a child, but did well as a writer and lived comfortably.

3 True.

4 False. Boucicault said he wanted…

Boucicault wrote 150 popular plays so he deserved a break. Dying is a break too far for most people, though.

5 True. Conrad was fed up because he'd lost all his money gambling. He shot himself but missed his heart and lived.

6 False. Wilde went to jail from 1895 till 1897. But he wrote the poem about the disgusting prison life in 1898 – a year *after* he came out of jail. Not a lot of people know that.

7 True. Know-it-all adults will tell you, 'It was *Rudyard* Kipling who wrote *The Jungle Book* in 1895.' And you can have great pleasure in telling them...

8 False. It must be false because William Wordsworth had NO sense of smell.

9 False. Trollope stood for Parliament and *lost*. The writer only got 740 votes. He said going around trying to get votes...

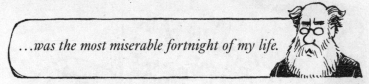

10 True. He used to dress the monkey as a woman and treat it like a lady. But one day the monkey became jealous of one of Swinburne's friends and tried to bite its master. The monkey was never seen again. Swinburne said he'd had it killed and grilled and eaten.

Foul fairs

The Victorians could be pretty bloodthirsty and cruel when it came to their idea of 'fun'. Dogs killing rats, or men boxing without gloves till their faces were bloody pulp – that was their 'fun'. Even the fairgrounds were cruel places. In between the swings and roundabouts were 'freak shows'. In the 1860s you really could go and could see these...

the
HYDE PARK FAIR
Presents
A SPECTACULAR TO CELEBRATE
QUEEN VICTORIA'S 30 YEARS
ON THE THRONE
SEE
THE TALENTED PIGS.
THE WORLD'S FATTEST MAN.
THE WORLD'S SPOTTIEST BOYS.
THE PONIES THAT TELL
YOUR FORTUNE.
MISS SCOTT-
THE TWO-HEADED LADY.
YORKSHIRE JACK-
THE LIVING SKELETON.
MADAM STEVENS-
THE PIG-FACED LADY

Now you may wonder what people really saw when they paid to see Madame Stevens, the Pig-faced Lady?

They saw a *bear* that:

- had its face and paws shaved;
- had its paws laced into padded gloves;
- was strapped to a chair with a table in front of it.

Then the performance began. The bear was asked questions. A boy prodded it with a stick after each question. The bear grunted and that seemed to be a reply...

- Are you 18 years old? (Prod – *Grunt.*)
- Is it true you were born in Preston in Lancashire? (Prod – *Grunt.*)
- Are you well and happy? (Prod – *Grunt.*)
- Are you planning to get married? (Prod – *Grunt.*)

But this was too cruel even for the Victorians and when the fair reached Clerkenwell it was banned.

Terrible timeline 1870s–1890s

Famous and Fortunate   *Forgotten and Failed*

1871

Henry Morton Stanley, famous Welsh explorer, sets off into the heart of Africa to find even-more-famous Scottish explorer David Livingstone. Sickly David refused to come home and died a couple of years later. But Stanley went on to report his adventures and became famous. His fortune came from working for the Belgian King Leopold, turning the African people into slaves with torture, whippings and chopping off bits of their bodies.

Sir Charles Dilke thinks Queen Vic is a bit of a waste of space. She shuts herself away and doesn't do anything useful. Charlie's answer? Get rid of the royal family and replace the Queen with a 'President' that everyone (well, every man) gets to vote for. Charlie wins a lot of support. But then Vic's son, Edward Prince of Wales, falls ill. People feel sorry for Vic and haven't the heart to throw her off the throne. Cheers for Charlie vanish and he is soon forgotten.

1874

Charles Kingsley wrote one of the first children's books, *The Water Babies*,

Thomas Castro, Australian butcher, turns up in England and he claims to be

which made him famous. A cheerful little story about ten-year-old Tom who suffers terribly as a chimney sweep. Tom falls into a river and drowns, but that's all right because he is changed into a fishy water baby. Just don't try jumping into a river if your cruel parent makes you sweep a chimney. This year Charles falls ill and dies soon after – but does NOT change into a water baby. Shame.

the long-lost son of Lady Tichborne. He also claims the long-lost son's fortune. Lady T's family can't bear to see their fortune go to a phoney! Tom is taken to court. He loses the case and gets 14 years' hard labour. Tough! But men, women and children are still working 14 hours a day in Victorian factories – so, even out of prison, many poor people do 'hard labour'. Like Tom, they are forgotten.

1879

Joseph Swan is a clever bloke from Sunderland, north-east England. Clever Joe invents something we all use millions of times in our lives – the electric light bulb. All right, it's not a very good one and it doesn't last long but it's a Victorian first. In New York, Thomas Edison makes a light bulb too. Joe Swan says

General Hutchinson should have stuck to being a general. Instead he gets a job with the government to check that bridges are safe. He checks the Tay Rail Bridge near Dundee – the longest bridge in the world at the time. 'It's fine!' says General Hutch. But on 28 December a storm

Tom pinched his idea. Tom Edison says Joe pinched his idea. Let's call it a draw. Joe goes on to be famous – but not as famous as Tom.

wrecks it and sends a train with a hundred passengers plunging 27 metres into the freezing water. The general isn't on the train. Shame.

IT'S NOT VERY GOOD AND IT DOESN'T LAST LONG, BUT IT WORKS

IT'S NOT VERY GOOD AND IT DOESN'T LAST LONG, BUT IT WAAAA

1881

Benjamin Disraeli dies but he has had a pretty successful life as a Prime Minister and as a writer of novels. What is the secret of his success? He was a creep. He kept telling Queen Victoria what a wonderful woman she was and she loved it – and she loved him. He came up with a super-duper idea to cheer up the miserable monarch. In 1877 he persuaded Parliament to make her 'Empress of India' as well as Queen. She was so pleased that she made Disraeli 'Lord Beaconsfield'. Fair swap.

Sir George Colley has been sent to sort out some troublesome Dutch farmers in South Africa – part of the British Empire. Sir G says the farmers (Boers) are 'feeble soldiers'. Easy job then? But at Majuba Hill these 'feeble' Boer soldiers beat his force of 1,500 'proper' soldiers. One of the Boers changes Sir G's mind. How did he do that, you ask? He puts a bullet through Sir G's forehead. And your mind doesn't get much more changed than that! Boers will cause Britain a lot of trouble for 20 years.

1888

Jack the Ripper is the most famous Victorian villain of all, yet no one knows his (or her) real name. Hundreds of clever writers have written hundreds of clever books to 'prove' dozens of suspects they think did it. But they can't all be right – unless there were dozens of Jack the Rippers working together in a team to chop up the eight victims. Some detectives think Jack was a doctor to Queen Vic, some think he was a relative of Victoria: a famous person who led a double life. As Jack might have said, 'Who nose?'

Dr Joseph Bell is a really clever feller. So clever that Joe's friend, a writer called Arthur Conan Doyle, makes him the star of a new detective book he has written. But Arthur doesn't call the detective Dr Joseph Bell. Oh, no. He gives the book detective a seriously weird name – Sherlock Holmes. Now Sherlock is the most famous detective never to have existed. Joe Bell, in the meantime, is not famous at all. Joe is very annoyed down there in his coffin. How do I know? Elementary, my dear reader.

1889

Robert Louis Stevenson retires to Samoa. This popular author is best known for his children's book, *Treasure Island*. He started by drawing a map of the imaginary island and used his friend W E Henley as the villain, Long John Silver. Would you make your friend into a villain? If you are a *Horrible Histories* reader then the answer is probably 'yes'. Anyway, Rob Lou knocked the book out in two weeks and said, 'It was to be a story for boys. Women were excluded.' Oo-er! Famous – among boys anyway.

Richard Pigott is a newspaper reporter and he wants a good story about the head of the Irish Parliament – Charles Parnell. So Richard makes one up. He says Parnell was part of the Phoenix Park Murder Plot in Dublin. And to prove it Richard has letters from Parnell ... except Richard wrote them himself. There is one problem with the forged letters – the spelling. The judges give Pigott a spelling test and the forger fails miserably. He is so bad that the judges fall about laughing. They must be teachers in their spare time.

1890

Cecil Rhodes, failed cotton grower, set up a diamond mine in South Africa and made his fortune. This year he becomes prime minister of

Joseph Carey Merrick – forgotten as Joe Merrick but, sadly, remembered as 'The Elephant Man'. At the age of five he got a disease that

the Cape Colony. He wants to make Africa into a British colony and make the British rich. Queen Vic loves that idea and thinks Rhodes is a star. Rhodes tricks the African natives out of their lands, upsets the Dutch (who also want to rob Africa of its riches) and generally gets Britain into the messy Boer Wars. But Cecil is all right.

swelled his head and feet; bags of brownish skin hang from his face while one arm grows almost like a flipper. He is locked in a workhouse but escapes – to a worse fate. Instead of showing him pity, villainous Victorians put him on show in fairgrounds for people to come and leer and jeer. Dr Treves rescued Joe but Joe dies this year at the age of 27.

1896

HG Wells is a writer with a great idea. Take all this science stuff that is going on in Victorian Britain and write stories about it. Last year he wrote *The Time Machine* and now he is working on an even wackier idea – *The Invisible Man*. He is even planning a book about an alien invasion from Mars, called *War of the Worlds*. A hundred years later and none of these things have

Ellis Roberts didn't enjoy a wonderful Victorian invention. A railway up Snowdon – the highest mountain in Wales – opens on 6 April this year. But at the opening two trains run out of control and crash into each other before they tumble over the Cwmglas cliff. Two hundred people survive and no one is killed – but pub owner Ellis Roberts hurts his

happened – but some people swear they have seen alien invaders. Blame Wells. He started it.

leg and it has to be cut off. Oops! The railway goes on to be a success, while Ellis and his leg are forgotten.

1899

Sir **Herbert Kitchener** is a British army commander. He likes to use machine guns to massacre enemies who don't have machine guns. In the Sudan (Africa) his Brit army killed 10,000 natives and lost only 28 Brits. Kitchener goes on fighting in South Africa against the Boers. He will be put in charge of the British army in the First World War. Then BOTH sides have machine guns – result? Millions dead. Thanks, Kitch.

Percy **Pilcher** is another of those brave Brits who has a dream of humans being able to fly. Percy has a glider, a bit like today's hang-gliders only not so strong. At Market Harborough in England a big crowd gather to watch him. If they are hoping for a disaster they get it. The tail falls off Percy's machine and he falls ten metres on to his head. Dead. Britain needed brave people like him – they died but they tried. Still, he is forgotten.

Talk like a villainous Victorian

Now you may think you're smarter than those villainous Victorian kids who never went to school (lucky kids!). And if you met one, they might struggle to understand you!

But the truth is *you*, with all your schooling, would find it just as hard to understand *them*!

You got that? No? Oh, well here's what those words mean...

Villainous Victorian Phrasebook

pudding-snammer	someone who steals from bakeries
snick fadger	someone who steals little coins
snow dropper	someone who steals washing hung out to dry
jerry sneak	someone who steals watches
river rat	someone who strips corpses found drowned in a river
fogle hunter	someone who steals silk handkerchiefs
Anabaptist	a thief who has been caught and thrown in a pond
back jumper	a burglar who goes through back doors
fagger	a small boy who can slip through a small window to let a burglar in
little snakesman	a fagger who slips through drains to get in a house
Tom Tug	mug or idiot
doddy	Scots for idiot
gump	Yorkshire for idiot
strut noddy	someone who doesn't know how stupid they really are
cracked the crib	broke into a house
yaffle	shout
ding on the coconut	bash on the head

twisted	killed
sturrabin	prison
pan	workhouse
staggering bob	scraps of meat
dogsbody	pease pudding
cod's head	fool
kiddy-nipped	pick-pocketed
spangle	money
wobbler	boiled leg of mutton

Getting the message

Victorian villains didn't just have their own speech. They had their own set of coded signs too.

Are you a door-to-door salesman (a 'hawker') going to call at that posh house and ask for some food or money? Better look at the sign chalked on the gatepost first. Your villainous friends have been there first and left a secret note...

Why not learn from history? Mark your teachers!

Criminal cures

Living in Victorian Britain was smelly, painful and cruel. Could you have survived even one single day?

The Victorians had some cures that would shock a modern doctor. For example, the chemical arsenic is a deadly poison – Victorian murderers loved to use it. But some people swallowed arsenic to cure their warts. (Swallow too much and you would never have to worry about your warts again!)

It cost a lot of money to visit a Victorian doctor. So parents would come up with their own (cheap) ways of treating their children.

Can you match these Victorian cases to their cures? Probably doesn't matter if you get them wrong – they wouldn't work anyway!

Household notes

PROBLEM

1. Ear ache
2. Dirty teeth
3. Rotten tooth
4. A Boil (big yellow spot)
5. A Cold
6. A sore throat
7. A cough
8. Chilblains (itchy blisters)
9. Tapeworms in the stomach
10. Warts

CURE

a) Fill it with rubber
b) Wrap a sweaty sock around the neck
c) Starve yourself, then fry some bacon
d) Rub with soot and salt
e) Drink a mix of beer, vinegar, black treacle and brown sugar
f) Bury string in the ground
g) Baked potato on the painful area
h) A bath in cold water every day
i) Wrap a red bandage round the neck
j) Slap on hot porridge

Answers:

1g) A potato would be baked in an oven, then wrapped in a scarf that was fastened round the head so the hot potato was against the ear. A baked onion would do if you  didn't have a potato handy. Some people said it worked!

2d) The salt works well as a tooth cleaner – not so sure about the soot. Would you want to kiss someone who'd cleaned their teeth in soot?

3a) The Victorians used a sort of rubber called 'gutta percha'. It was used for toys and golf balls. It went soft in boiling water so all you had to do was heat it, bung it in the hole in the tooth, then let it set. Useless!

4j) A cure for boils was to put on something hot, wrapped in cloth – a 'poultice'. Porridge oats would work – but you could use mashed carrots, a slice of wet bread, a cloth soaked in vinegar (if you want to smell like a chip shop) or hot beer (if you want to smell like a pub).

5b) Phew! But true. The scent of a mouldy sock was supposed to clear the head. The Victorians also put wet salt in the hand and sniffed hard. It was supposed to help with a blocked nose – but if your nose was sore it would be very painful. 'Snot nice. Better to sniff and suffer. Or you could try one of these other useless cold cures...

- Soak your feet in hot water with mustard.
- Roast a goose and scoop out the grease to rub into your back and chest.
- Drink hot whisky.

6i) For some reason the bandage had to be red. The usual material was a wool stuff called flannel. Cosy. But a cure? I think not.

7e) Boil them all together for 20 minutes, then add a small bottle of rum. Have a teaspoon of the mixture three times a day. Yeuch! Let's face it – if YOU had a cough, and someone threatened to give you a dose of that lot, you'd soon stop coughing. Perfect cure!

8h) Nice, eh? Especially in winter. If you got the dreaded chilblains on your feet, then you could slap wet bread on them. That's a bit awkward if you fancy a game of football.

9c) These jolly little worms live in your gut and feed on your food. So all you have to do is starve yourself and you starve the worm. Now comes the clever bit – fry some bacon and the smell will drive the hungry little parasite mad. It will leap out of your mouth to get at the bacon. You got him! Unless he gets the bacon first, turns round and gets you!

10f) Bury one piece of string for each wart. As the string rots then the wart rots away. That's a lot of rot. Another trick was to rub your wart with a piece of steak, put the steak in a matchbox and bury it. Don't stake your life on it working.

Quacks for the Queen

Victoria was potty about her husband, Albert. Then Albert died. She was so miserable that she refused to be seen in public for years. Victoria photographed every part of the room where Albert died to make sure nothing would change – so she could pretend he hadn't died. A jug of hot water was placed in his room each day. His dressing gown was laid on his bed each night. She even had a cast made of his hand and kept a copy so she could hold hands with him.

The doctors couldn't make her happy – so they gave her happy drugs (laudanum). Before long, Queen Vic was a drug addict.

While sad Vic swallowed her happy drugs, the poor people in Britain had no pill for their sicknesses…

Singing the blues

The disease 'cholera' was caused by drinking dirty water full of human poo and pee. In 1849, 54 people from London's slums wrote to *The Times* newspaper about their terrible toilets – or 'privies' as they called them. The cholera must have affected their spelling too, because here's what they wrote…

> Sir,
> We live in muck and filth. We ain't got no privez, no dust bins, no water splies and no drain or suer in the whole place. If the Colera comes Lord help us.

Test your teacher

Teachers are clever people. Far too clever to read a *Horrible Histories* book. So keep this one hidden in case they stumble across it and see the answers to the villainous questions you are going to ask them about the Victorian age. Here we go…

1 A potato famine hit Scotland in the 1840s and hundreds died. One of the men sent to help them had the right name for the job. What was he called?
a) Ivor Cornhill (I've a hill of corn, geddit?)
b) Pine Coffin
c) Scot Feeder

2 Sir Robert Peel created the police force, but the bobbies couldn't stop him dying in a traffic accident. How did he die?
a) He was crushed under the wheels of a carriage while crossing the road. Splat!!!
b) He was crossing a railway line when a train hit his coach. Splinter!!!
c) He fell off his horse and the horse fell on top of him. Scrunch!!!

3 In 1875 the first one was opened in London. First what?
a) Roller-skating rink
b) Ice-skating rink
c) Bottle of ink

4 In 1876 William Gladstone lost his job as prime minister to old enemy Benjamin Disraeli. So now he spends his time writing a book! What does he write?

a) A book on how to become a great prime minister, just like him. Boastful.

b) A fairy story for children with a man like Disraeli as the wicked wizard. Revengeful.

c) A horrible history book. Dreadful.

5 Queen Victoria's son, Edward, got married. One guest at the wedding was a three-year-old German prince. What did he do that caused a bit of trouble?

a) He was supposed to carry the 'train' at the back of the bride's dress. But he had stuffed himself with sweets and threw up all over it.

b) He was guarded by two princes because he was so naughty and he bit their legs to try to escape.

c) The archbishop, in his tall hat and fine robes, walked past and the prince stuck out a foot and tripped him up. The archbishop died and the wedding was put off.

6 How did some Victorians try to discover the name of a thief who robbed them?

a) They called in Sherlock Holmes – great brain.

b) They baked a toad in a ball of clay – great pain.

c) They went to church and prayed for God to strike the thief with lightning – not sane.

7 The Gloucester hangman liked to show off at public executions to give the crowd a laugh. What did he do?

a) He tap-danced on the scaffold while the crowd waited for the prisoner to arrive – a bit of a jig.

b) He wore a black hood over his head but put false hair on top of it – a bit of a wig.

c) He let the victim drop, then twirled the rope – a bit of a pig.

8 A train crash in Wales left 33 passengers dead. What did their train hit?

a) A couple of petrol wagons. The passengers fried – boom and sizzle.

b) The wall of a dam. The passengers drowned – bang and drizzle.

c) A lorry carrying fireworks. The passengers exploded – whoosh and fizzle.

9 In the 1860s women were wearing wide skirts called 'crinolines'. Very fashionable. One big problem. What?

a) The crinoline material could be itchy. As Victorian women wore no knickers, they spent half their lives trying not to scratch their bottoms.

b) The crinoline material was made from the skin of very rare white badgers and they became extinct by 1873 when the last one was shot.

c) The skirts were very wide at the bottom and could easily get too near a coal fire. Crinoline burned fast and furious, and several women were burned to death in accidents.

10 Top actress Sarah Bernhardt had a curious habit. What?
a) She liked to have a bath in the milk of 20 black asses.
b) She liked to sleep in a coffin each night.
c) She liked to polish her false teeth with white boot polish to make them shine.

Answers:

1b) Sir Edward Pine Coffin was given the job of making sure the extra food supplies were shared out in Scotland. Of course, the starved Scots didn't use pine coffins – they were just buried in blankets.

2c) In July 1850 Bob Peel was riding up Constitution Hill in London when he fell and his horse fell on top of him. This was not good for his health. Do not try it at home – or on Constitution Hill.

UURH. YOU'VE SAT IN SOMETHING SQUISHY

3a) Roller skates had been invented over a hundred years before but this was the first 'rink' to be built. Back in 1760 skates were worn by Joseph Merlin to a musical party. He skated into the ballroom, playing a violin. Sadly he lost control, skated into a £500 mirror, smashed it, smashed his violin and almost cut himself to shreds.

4c) *The Bulgarian Horrors* is about the terrible Turkish torturers that had attacked the helpless Bulgarian people. The book was a huge success, selling 200,000 copies in a week. But Gladstone went back to Parliament and became prime minister again. Well, being prime minister is easier than being an author ... as any author will tell you.

5b) Little Prince Wilhelm of Germany was 'guarded' by two English princes because he was so naughty. And little Prince W did not want to be guarded, so he dropped off his seat in church, crawled along the floor and bit the legs of his guards. This charming child grew up to be Kaiser Wilhelm who led Germany into the First World War against Britain. Millions died. Shame he didn't just stick to biting legs.

6b) In the Middle Ages the peasants believed this old magic worked. They baked a toad in a ball of clay, then broke open the clay; they believed the toad would scratch the name of the thief before it died. Amazingly some people in Victorian England still believed this nonsense.

7c) Not only did he spin the corpse on the end of the rope, he also slapped it on the back and shook hands with it. He pretended to have a chat to it and all the while the audience were laughing.

8a) The train was travelling from Chester to Holyhead when it hit a couple of petrol tankers. The passengers were swallowed by a fireball. Horrible.
9c)

10b) Sleeping in a coffin was fine so long as nobody came along and nailed the lid down. Sarah also kept a cheetah as a pet.

Top ten villainous Victorians

Victorian villains were greedy, ruthless, cruel and didn't care who they hurt. Some villains were poor people robbing other poor people. But some were rich and robbing everyone – filthy rich. Or just plain filthy. There were thousands of these villains and you could write a hundred top tens. But here is a *Horrible Histories* top ten.

10 Theophile Marzials
Charge: Murdering the English language
Theo was a poet who made hundreds of people suffer when he started reading his poems. One of the worst was the poem he called 'A Tragedy'. Next time your teacher asks you to read your favourite poem to the class, then make them all suffer with this codswallop...

Death! Plop.
The barges down the river flop.
Flop, plop!
The oozy waters that lounge and flop
On the black scrag-piles where the loose cords plop,
As the raw wind whines in the thin tree-top.
Plop, plop.
At the water that oozes up, plop and plop,
On the barges that flop
And dizzy me dead.
I might reel and drop.
Plop Dead.
Drop Dead.
Flip. Flop Plop.

Villainometer rating: 2/10

9 William Foster

Charge: Cruelty to children for over 130 years

Up until 1869 parents could send their children to school IF they wanted to – and IF there was a school in the area. Then in 1870 wicked William Foster came up with a horrific idea – school for everyone and everyone will be *forced* to go!!!

There are a hundred ways that young people learn – Will decided that packing a bunch of kids into the same room to learn the same thing at the same time is the best. And today's young people are still stuck with that wacky idea. Cruel or what?

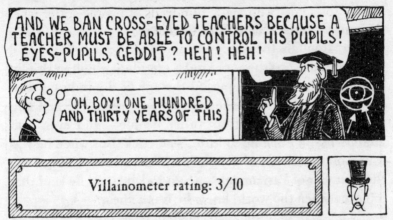

AND WE BAN CROSS-EYED TEACHERS BECAUSE A TEACHER MUST BE ABLE TO CONTROL HIS PUPILS! EYES-PUPILS, GEDDIT? HEH! HEH!

OH, BOY! ONE HUNDRED AND THIRTY YEARS OF THIS

Villainometer rating: 3/10

8 Justice Blackborough

Crime: Using the law to make money

Justice Blackborough was a judge. He was paid well for being a judge but he was greedy. He was paid more every time someone was set free on 'bail' – when arrested, people paid him money so they didn't have to stay in jail while they waited for a trial. Every time Blackborough gave someone 'bail' he was paid two shillings and four pence – a week's wage for a poor flower-seller. So Blackborough simply had dozens of innocent people arrested, gave them bail and pocketed the money.

Villainometer rating: 4/10

7 George Hudson (the 'Railway King')
Charge: Robbing the rich.
Georgie had over a thousand miles of railways built in Britain and made the Victorian period the age of the railways. But his main aim was to make himself very rich. He lied and cheated to get money from other people – and even sold land that didn't belong to him. Neat trick. But when he was found out hundreds of people lost their money. George was the Member of Parliament for Sunderland, and he kept that job even when the world knew he was a cheat.

Villainometer rating: 6/10

6 Mr Sneyd-Kynnersley

Crime: Cruelty to children

Mr S-K was head teacher at a public school in Victorian England. One of his pupils was the artist Roger Fry who described Sneyd-Kynnersley's beatings of the boys. Roger Fry had to help the horrible headmaster with the floggings...

In the middle of Sneyd-Kynnerley's room was a large box covered in black cloth. The victim was told to take down his trousers and lean over the block while I and another boy held him down. The swishing was given with the master's full strength and it only took two or three strokes for drops of blood to form everywhere. It continued for 15 or 20 strokes by which time the wretched boy's bottom was a mass of blood. Generally the boys took it in silence but sometimes there were scenes of screaming and howling and struggling, which made me almost sick with disgust.

And that wasn't the worst. There was a wild, red-haired, Irish boy, a cruel brute himself, who was punished. Either it was

> deliberate or he had diarrhoea, but he
> let fly. The angry headmaster, instead of
> stopping, went on with even more fury till
> the ceiling and the walls of his room
> were covered with filth.

Villainometer rating: 6.5/10

And you thought your teacher was bad?

5 Lord MacDonald

Crime: Robbing the poor and needy

The MacDonald clan were starving in the 1848 Scottish famine, but there was cheap food for them in Liverpool. 'I will buy it!' said the Scottish chieftain, Lord Mac. He bought it – then sold it for twice as much as he'd paid. Lord MacDonald pocketed the money, while his people starved.

I COULD MURDER A MACDONALD!

Villainometer rating: 7/10

120

4 Queen Victoria's government

Crime: Making poor people's life a misery

It was the government that made the laws. But the government was run by the rich people, so the laws they made were for the rich. (The government even started a war in China to *look after* rich British drug dealers.)

When there was suffering it was the ordinary people who suffered. The poor were punished for petty crimes – even children – and were left to rot in slums and die of disease.

And the government could be criminally useless too. They sent men off to fight in the Crimean War against Russia, but...

Villainometer rating: 7/10

3 Dr Neill Cream

Crime: Serial killing

For some reason the Victorian age was the age of the poisoner, and Neill Cream was one of the deadliest. Dr Cream went to prison in the United States for murdering three women and a man. But they released him so he could come to Britain and kill still more. (Thanks, America.)

He offered tablets to girls saying they would make them really lovely – they made them really dead instead.

He then offered to help the police to catch the killer. He seems to have had a twisted sense of humour. He emptied the posh Metropole Hotel in London by printing and sending out a notice to all the guests. It read…

Ellen Donworth's Death
To the guests of the Metropole Hotel

Ladies and Gentlemen,

I hereby notify you that the person who poisoned Ellen Donworth on the 13th of October last year is today working at the Metropole. Your lives are in danger as long as you stay in this hotel.

Yours faithfully,

W H Murray

London, April 1892

As Cream was hanged he cried, 'I am Jack the Ripper!' However, when Jack the Ripper was killing girls in London, Neill Cream was in prison in America – so he must have used a very long knife to chop them. Still, Cream probably killed more people than the famous Ripper, and his victims died more slowly and in more pain.

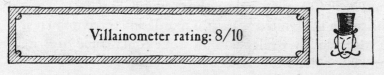

Villainometer rating: 8/10

2 Lord Londonderry
Crime: Slavery

The Londonderry family owned lots of land in the north of England. When coal was found on their land they made a fortune selling it. But the men, women and children who did the digging and the dying to get that coal were treated like slaves.

- Lord Londonderry made £61,364 in a year from selling coal. His miners were lucky to make £8 a year. The miners hated the Londonderry family. Wonder why?
- The miners went on strike for more money. Lord Londonderry threw them out of their homes and brought in other cheap workers to keep his money coming in.
- When there was an explosion at a colliery, the mine managers blocked off the mineshaft so the coal could be saved. The men underground were left to die.
- A disaster killed 95 men in one of his pits and the poor miners' wives and children were paid just one week's wages for their dead husbands. The rest of the town raised £4265 for the families. Lord Londonderry refused to give a penny.

123

- A writer later turned the tale into a poem…

> *The hundred men of Haswell, all died on that same day;*
> *They all died in the same hour; all died the self-same way.*
> *'Oh you rich man of Haswell, now help us, please,' they cried.*
> *A full week's wage he paid them for every man who died.*
> *And when the wage was given, his rich chest locked up he;*
> *The iron lock clicked sharply, the women wept bitterly.*

GIVE MORE? NO WAY! I MIGHT LOSE SOME OF MY SIXTY-ONE THOUSAND, THR… etc

Villainometer rating: 9/10

1 Queen Victoria

Crime: Robbery

Victoria took the throne and all the wealth that went with it. While most of her people had to work hard to earn their money, Victoria did nothing. In fact, after her dear husband died she spent 40 years hidden away from the people she was supposed to lead … but still took the money, of course.

Taking money you haven't earned? Isn't that robbery?

We were very much amused

That's all right then. She was amused, while millions of her people slaved in the mines and the factories, shivered in the slums and the workhouses, and starved with the poverty and the famines.

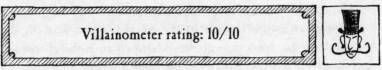

Villainometer rating: 10/10

Epilogue

In 1901 Queen Victoria died and her son, Edward VII, took the throne. He was 59 years old and was beginning to think the old Queen would never kick the bucket.

A lot of things changed in the 63 years she was on the throne – at the start people were hanged in public, women and children worked down mines, and doctors wore mucky black coats to operate on patients.

At the end there were motor cars, a massive British Empire and machine guns. (The last two killed millions in the 20th century, but the first is catching up fast.)

There were still slums, wars, disease and crime when Edward came to the throne. There still are…

Victorian Prime Minister Benjamin Disraeli said Victoria did not rule over *one* nation – she ruled over *two* nations.

- Two groups of people who each didn't understand how the other one lived or thought or felt.
- Two groups of people who ate different food, had different ways and even lived under different laws.
- Two groups of people who might have been from different planets…

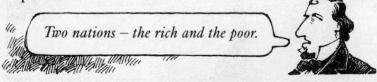

Two nations – the rich and the poor.

Many of the poor were villainous. To stay alive, they *had* to be. They robbed and rioted, grabbed and garrotted, stabbed and stole in a world of hangings and hatred, disease and easy death.

Many of the rich were villainous. They had to be to cling on to what they had. There were cheating chieftains and beating teachers who made slaves of servants and delighted in drink and drugs.

The two nations often hated one another. The writer G W Reynolds knew which was the worst. In his book, *The Sailor's Wife*, one of his characters raves...

There is no class in the world as heartless as the English upper class. Even when they give money to the poor they are only giving back a tiny part of the massive wealth they have made from the poor. They made it from the blood and the muscles of the wretched, slaving, starving millions.

HEARTLESS UPPER CLASS?

I CAN'T THINK WHAT HE COULD MEAN

VILLAINOUS VICTORIANS

GRISLY QUIZ

Now find out if you're a Villainous Victorian expert!

QUICK QUESTIONS

1. In 1830 the Liverpool to Manchester railway opened. How did Liverpool MP William Huskisson celebrate? (Clue: it's a knockout)

2. In 1831 the north-eastern port of Sunderland brought in a new import. What? (Clue: dis eez a horrible thing to suffer)

3. In 1842 women were banned from doing something they had been doing for hundreds of years. What? (Clue: mine, all mine!)

4. In 1844 a lady wrote that people were pleased when they smelled bad drains. Why? (Clue: red sky at night)

5. In 1846 a 16-year-old boy was charged with travelling on a train on a 12-year-old's half-price ticket. What was his excuse? (Clue: time to grow)

6. London 'toshers' waded though sewage every day – up to 1.5 metres of the stuff. Why? (Clue: a golden opportunity)

7. In 1847 the Irish were crowding on to 'coffin ships'. Why? (Clue: they've had their chips)

8. In 1848 many European countries were in revolt. The British rebels, the Chartists, had a rally in London but it was a failure. Why? (Clue: it's a wash out)

9. In 1852 in London a small room is opened for men in

Fleet Street and they are very relieved! Why? (Clue: gents still use them)

10. In 1853, Australia got stroppy and refused to take any more from Britain. What? (Clue: if they're barred from Australia they'll be barred in Britain)

11. In 1855 Florence Nightingale was nursing Brit soldiers who were fighting the Russians. What happened to their amputated limbs? (Clue: it will make you pig sick)

12. Punching opponents and gouging their eyes was banned in which sport in 1863? (Clue: players put their foot in it)

13. Irish rebels in 1866 invaded which British territory? (Clue: they mountied a successful defence)

14. In 1869 sailors were banned from wearing what? (Clue: it's a close shave)

15. When this man died in 1870 it was said he was 'exhausted by fame'. Who was he? (Clue: no more Christmas Carols)

16. In 1870 a new law forced everyone to do it, even poor little children. What? (Clue: you had to join the class war)

17. In 1879 the Tay Bridge collapsed and a train with almost 100 passengers sank. The bridge inspector had said it was safe. How many bridges had he inspected before? (Clue: not enough)

18. In 1880 the famous writer George Eliot died. What's unusual about him? (Clue: he isn't)

19. SS *Daphne* was launched on the river Clyde and the workers got a huge surprise. What? (Clue: duck!)

20. In 1888 the police named a murderer even though they never caught him (or her). Who? (Clue: and Jill?)

21. In 1890 a man died. He had been cruelly put on show to the ghoulish public because of his unusual illness. It made him look like what? (Clue: big ears)

22. Copy-cat Blackpool built a copy of the Eiffel Tower in 1894. But is the Blackpool Tower bigger or smaller than the French one? (Clue: it's one or the other!)

23. In 1896 Londoners saw 'Boxing Kangaroos' in Australia. How? (Clue: somebody shot the kangaroos)

24. In 1896 motorists were glad to see the back of a rule that slowed them down. What rule? (Clue: they weren't glad to see the back of this man)

25. In 1899 Percy Pilcher fell 10 metres and was killed. What did he fall from? (Clue: he was hanging around)

26. Queen Victoria's son-in-law, Prince Christian, lost an eye in a shooting accident. At dinner parties he entertained guests with his collection of what? (Clue: quite a sight)

Behave like a Victorian

If a time machine dropped your dad in Victorian London would he act like a gentleman ... or a slob? Test him with these 'do' and 'don't' problems taken from a book of Gentlemen's Manners and see if he could have been accepted by polite Victorians. Just one problem ... if he makes a single mistake he could well be frowned on for the rest of his life!

Do or don't...

1. offer your hand to an older person to be shaken.
2. eat from the side of your soup spoon and not the end.
3. write to people you know on post cards.
4. remove your overcoat before you enter someone's living room.
5. use slang words.
6. bite into your bread at dinner.
7. call your servants 'girls'.
8. raise your hat to a lady in the street.
9. spit on the pavement.
10. sit with legs crossed.

Quick Questions

1. Huskisson stepped from his carriage to say hello to friends, was hit by a train and died.

2. The disease of cholera. Not only does it give you disgusting diarrhoea but victims turn blue before they die. 20,000 died in the next year.

3. Women (and boys under 10) were no longer allowed to work in mines. They lost their wages so it isn't all good news.

4. It was a sign of bad weather on the way. People were glad of the warning. Modern weather forecasts smell better.

5. 'The train's so slow, I was 12 when I got on it.' On most lines 30 mph was thought to be quite fast enough.

6. They were looking for coins and metal dropped through drains. Would you stick your hand down a toilet for your pocket money? Toshers would.

7. They were emigrating from Ireland because they were starving in the potato famine. The old ships, nicknamed coffin ships, didn't always make it. Starve or drown? Some choice.

8. It rained heavily and many people stayed at home rather than get wet.

9. It was the first flushing public toilet for men – but not women, who would have to keep their legs crossed!

10. Convicts. Australia was a dumping ground for Brit criminals and now it stopped. Brit criminals got harsher sentences at home instead and no kangaroo steaks.

11. They were dumped outside the hospital and eaten by pigs. Then the pigs were eaten by the patients ... including the patients who lost arms and legs. You could say they

ended up eating themselves! Yeuch!

12. Soccer. The new rules said that only the goalkeeper could handle the ball. It also banned fighting on the pitch. Someone should tell today's players!

13. Canada! Yes it sounds odd but with the help of US troops the Irish rebels attacked Brit troops in Canada as the first stage of attacking Brit troops in Ireland.

14. Moustaches. Sailors could be clean shaven or wear beards, but moustaches were popular with soldiers and the navy didn't want its men to look like their great rivals in the army!

15. Charles Dickens. He was only 58 but was racing around the country, reading and acting his characters. It killed him.

16. Go to school. The Education Reform Act forced everyone to suffer at school whether they liked it or not.

17. None. The inspector wasn't trained and had never inspected a bridge before. He wouldn't have known a bad bridge if it had jumped up and bitten him on the nose.

18. George Eliot was a woman, real name Mary Anne Evans. She didn't think publishers would print a book by a woman so she lied and said she was a man.

19. The ship slid into the river, rolled over and drowned 124 of them. Well, they built it, so they couldn't complain – and they didn't.

20. Jack the Ripper. He killed eight women and the mystery has never been forgotten – or solved. But Queen Victoria showed an unusual interest in the case. Hmmmm!

21. An elephant. Joseph Merrick was known as the Elephant Man and he was treated as a freak, rather than a sick person. He died aged just 27.

22. Smaller. Blackpool Tower is only half the height of the Eiffel Tower – but people falling off the top end up with

exactly the same amount of deadness.

23. The kangaroos were in the first cinema show in Britain. Now you know the answer you'll be hoppy.

24. Motorists were now allowed to drive without being led by a man with a red flag. The speed limit also went up from 4 mph to 20 mph. Scary!

25. An early hang glider.

26. Glass eyes. His favourite was a bloodshot eye which he used when he had a cold!

Behave like a Victorian

1. Don't. Wait until they have offered it to you.

2. Do. And remember you mustn't gurgle or suck in your breath while you sip your soup.

3. Don't. Write letters or nothing at all.

4. Do. Even if it's only a very short call.

5. Don't. Well, usually. There are some slang words that a gentleman may use. If you don't know what they are then avoid slang altogether.

6. Don't. Break off a piece and place it in your mouth.

7. Don't. Call them maids or servants.

8. Do. BUT ... wait till she has bowed to you first and do not wave your hat in the air the way the French do – put it straight back on to your head.

9. Don't. Or anywhere else for that matter!

10. Don't. The book admits that most men do this but says it is extremely impolite.

INTERESTING INDEX

Where will you find 'chilblains',
'pig-faced lady' and 'squirters' in an index?
In a Horrible Histories book, of course!

Peel, Robert (British police founder) 58, 109
Phoenix Park Murder Plot 96
pickpockets 5, 13, 27, 43, 65
picture shows, moving 83
pig-faced lady 91
Pigott, Richard (British reporter) 96
Pilcher, Percy (British glider pilot) 98
plays, petrifying 78–83
police 13, 15, 26, 58–67, 103, 109, 122
poo 19, 108
poultices (cloth-wrapped cures) 106
prisons 20, 23–5, 71–2, 88
privies (toilets) 108
pubs 79, 97, 106
punishments, putrid 16–17, 21–3, 71–2
puppets, peeping at 78–9

railway tracks 80, 97–8, 118
rats 34, 70, 90
Reynolds, G.W. (British writer) 127
Rhodes, Cecil (British colonialist) 96–7

schools 33, 36–42
shot drill (prison punishment) 21–2
slaves 79, 81, 92, 123, 125, 127
slums 5, 13, 31, 54, 61, 108, 121, 125–6
Snow, John (British doctor) 54
squirters (pistols) 13
Stanley, Henry Morton (Welsh explorer) 92
Stevenson, Robert Louis (Scottish novelist) 96
Swan, Joseph (English inventor) 93–4
Swinburne, Algernon (British poet) 87, 89

tapeworms, in gut 104, 107
Tennyson, Alfred (English poet) 86
theatre 78
toads, baked in clay 111, 113–14
transportation 30–4, 54

Trollope, Anthony (English novelist) 87, 89

Victoria (British queen) 5–6, 8–11, 13, 31, 41, 43, 45–6, 52, 54–5, 57–8, 92, 95–7, 107, 124–6
villains 116–25

warts, cures for 104, 107
Wells, H.G. (English novelist) 86, 97–8
whips 17, 20, 92
Wilde, Oscar (British playwright/poet) 86, 88
Wilhelm (German kaiser/chief) 113
women
  killer 72–7
  mistreated 68, 74, 78
  working 126
Wordsworth, William (English poet) 87, 89
workhouses 27, 97, 102, 125

139

Terry Deary was born at a very early age, so long ago he can't remember. But his mother, who was there at the time, says he was born in Sunderland, north-east England, in 1946 – so it's not true that he writes all *Horrible Histories* from memory. At school he was a horrible child only interested in playing football and giving teachers a hard time. His history lessons were so boring and so badly taught, that he learned to loathe the subject. *Horrible Histories* is his revenge.

Martin Brown was born in Melbourne, on the proper side of the world. Ever since he can remember he's been drawing. His dad used to bring back huge sheets of paper from work and Martin would fill them with doodles and little figures. Then, quite suddenly, with food and water, he grew up, moved to the UK and found work doing what he's always wanted to do: drawing doodles and little figures.

Make sure you've got the whole horrible lot!

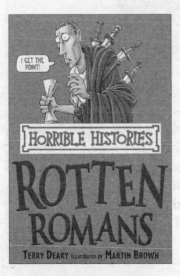

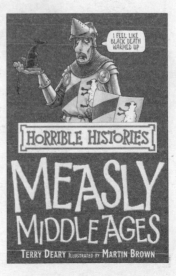